Claude Hervé-Bazin

JPMGUIDES

the taste of Portugal

CONTENTS

botanical surprises

stylish glimpses of the past

island secrets to share

MADEIRA AND THE AZORES

Before the discovery of America, medieval sailors had reached the shores of these enigmatic Atlantic isles crowned with cones and mist-wreathed peaks, their dark sheer cliffs plunging into the deep blue froth-fringed ocean. They appeared on some charts but had not been named, and were surrounded by a halo of mystery.

Poets alluded to distant legends: these were, perhaps, the remains of Atlantis, the domain of Atlas, son of Neptune, who inherited them when the gods shared out the world. Fabulous Atlantis, that Plato located "beyond the Pillars of Hercules, in the middle of the Atlantic Ocean". It was said that the mythical continent had sunk into the depths of the Sete Cidades caldeira on São Miguel, in the Azores. Inspired by wonder mingled with fear, the fables surrounding the islands suggested they could be the last home of the blessed, paradise on earth—or the fount of all evil. Surely the gateway to Hell was on the Azores—as proved by the satanic fumes issuing forth from the bowels of the earth.

Between Old World and New

Madeira first appeared on the map during the golden age of the great explorers. Along with the Azores, it was the last outpost of Europe, a Christian watchtower guarding the route to the new world. The island became the pivot of early voyages to the west coast of Africa, to India, Malacca and Macao, the Moluccas and to America. It was a welcome stopover, where the ships could take on stores and the crews could disembark and recover from the rigours of a dangerous voyage. Some of these early visitors decided to stay.

Over the years, this haven midway between America and Europe gave birth to a new culture. Its links to Portugal, its language and traditional hospitality cannot be denied, but the Madeiran identity sets it apart. Politically, both Madeira and the Azores have a great deal of autonomy.

People from all over the world have contributed in some measure to the island. Portuguese adventurers returning from America built baroque churches and covered them in *azulejos* tiles. From the continent came the heady *saudade* and bullfighting. Slaves brought from Cape Verde to work the sugar plantations have also left their mark. The windmills look as though they were transplanted from the Netherlands; many of the buildings are unmistakably British, and a faint Victorian atmosphere recalls the close ties between England and Madeira in the 19th century. To all this, add the subtle spices that were brought from the four corners of the world in the bags of pirates, occupants and traders.

A People of Character

Fervent Catholics, inordinately fond of feast-making, the islanders are famed for their strength of character. Until recent times, they used to go whaling in simple rowing boats—a typical example of their fearlessness. Outward-looking yet firmly attached to the land, they are proudly self-sufficient and insular by nature. Each community, each tiny hamlet has nurtured and scrupulously preserved its own separate identity.

The first settlers were skilful farmers and cleared the original forest to make the island habitable. They planted a patchwork of gardens stepping up the steep slopes, protected from the wind by regiments of low stone walls. Only about a third of Madeira's land can be cultivated by hand in this way, yet its possibilities have been exploited to the full: terraces of bananas; vines entwining the limbs of high-perched fruit trees; corn, cabbages and carrots growing between their roots. Every last patch of land is used, irrigated by an ingenious system of *levadas*, channels that collect and distribute the water coursing down from the mountains.

The land may be fertile, but the practical difficulties of working the soil, together with the hazards of earthquake, tidal waves and poverty, made willing emigrants of the Madeirans and Azoreans. Thousands of islanders set out every year in hope of a better future in the New World. In all, over a million Madeirans left their island—four times more than its resident population. A third of them settled in South Africa, others in North America or Venezuela. And more than 350,000 Azoreans moved to Brazil, Canada, Hawaii or New England, where their forebears hunted whales in the 19th century. However, since Portugal entered the European Union, the recent development of the islands in general, and of tourism in particular, seems to have reversed this tendency. Expatriate islanders are returning to their homeland, in search of a quieter life.

The Islands

The archipelago, of volcanic origin, is actually closer to the coast of Morocco than to Lisbon, 1,000 km (620 miles) away. Apart from Madeira itself, the group also includes the island of Porto Santo to the northeast and the uninhabited Desertas and Selvagens, near the Canary Islands. The nine isles of the Azores, spread over almost 600 km (370 miles), are divided into three separate groups. Santa Maria and São Miguel, where the capital, Ponta Delgada, is located, are the closest to Europe. The central group includes Terceira, Graciosa, São Jorge, Pico and Faial. Finally, far to the northwest are Flores, with the highest rainfall, and Corvo. Flores lies 1,800 km (1,120 miles) from Lisbon.

Nature has been wildly extravagant with flowers. The plants introduced by settlers have not confined themselves to the gardens but have spread unhindered, surging over the balconies, carpeting the windows and creeping down to the edges of the roads. In February, the camellias burst into bloom, followed by clouds of azaleas in late spring; in summer, purple bougainvillaea cascades over ancient walls, mimosa fills the air with its scent and jacaranda petals carpet the streets in blue. Flame trees shade the village squares, amaryllis, birds of paradise, hibiscus and hydrangea turn the island into an exotic Garden of Eden.

Huber/Lawrence

Dressed in roses and a smile for the spring Flower Festival.

These bucolic islands appeal to painters and romantics alike. As you travel their narrow, winding roads, images of the Europe of yesterday come to mind. Houses of basalt, their doors and windows the shade of the sky, of dark wine, of the sun, melt into the landscape, their rich colours echoed in the gardens of Madeira's country estates, in the velvet green of the mountains, the ochres of the cliffs and the sparkling blue sea.

Thatched with straw, the little A-frame houses at Santana have served farmers for centuries, as dwellings or cattle byres.

hemis.fr/Barbier

FLASHBACK

The story goes that Madeira was first inhabited at some time in the 14th century by an English merchant, Robert Machin, who had eloped from Bristol with his mistress, Anne d'Arfet, and was shipwrecked there. Though Anne died, Robert eventually escaped on a raft. Apparently he related his discovery to a Spanish slave, and news of the island spread from there.

There are many variations on the same tale, but whatever the truth, the Medici Atlas of 1351 clearly marks an Isola della Legna—Isle of Wood—off the coast of Portugal. In 1418, when Prince Henry the Navigator sent explorers João Gonçalves Zarco ("one-eyed") and Tristão Vaz Teixeira to reconnoitre the west coast of Africa, they were blown off course by a storm, ran aground on Porto Santo and observed a large, forested island to the southwest which they called Ilha de Madeira, island of trees. Damage made good, they returned to Portugal to take on fresh supplies and returned to claim Madeira the following year, landing at a place Zarco named Machico.

Madeira and Porto Santo were declared a province of Portugal in 1425, becoming the first rung on the long ladder of the Portuguese colonial empire. Two years later, in 1427, a mariner named Diego de Silves explored another group of islands far to the northwest. On August 15, 1432, Brother Gonçalo Velho landed in his turn with a small group on an uninhabited isle which he called Santa Maria. This soldier-monk had been sent by Henry to exorcise the islands, believed to be haunted by the devil. The archipelago was named the Azores, the sailors mistaking the kites circling overhead for goshawks, a bird known as *açor* in Portuguese (and never seen on these islands).

Colonization

The first thing the colonists did on Madeira was to clear the land by burning the forest. It's said that the fire blazed continuously for seven years, and when it finally died out, the centuries-old leaf mould had turned into rich and fertile soil. Meanwhile, the inhabitants had found refuge in a valley, on the banks of what became the Ribeira dos Socorridos (Survivors' River). When the flames finally died down, Zarco, who had become captain-donatory of the island, began to plan colonization. Wheat was planted to supply Lisbon. In 1425 a settlement was founded on the bay of Funcho (fennel), where Funchal now stands. A first contingent was shipped in—Moorish slaves and impoverished peasants from the Algarve. In 1439 they were joined by criminals from Portugal's gaols along with Jewish and Breton families, and sent to found the first colonies on the islands of Santa Maria, São Miguel and Terceira. Henry's sister, the Duchess of Burgundy and Flanders, sent a group of Flemish pioneers who, by 1490, formed a small community on Faial. Cattle were introduced, sugar cane planted, and more slaves brought from the Canary Islands and Cape Verde. On Madeira, the first sugar mill was built in 1452 and the island, under the control of Flemish merchants and the great Portuguese landowners, entered a period of prosperity. Ships laden with sugar set sail for Portugal, France and England. Henry sent stocks of the Malvasia vine from Crete which were planted on terraces hacked out of the mountainsides. Soon the production of wine began.

On the Route of the Explorers

Alvise Ca' da Mosto, a Venetian in the pay of Portugal, was one of the first to put into port here on his way to the Cape Verde islands in 1455. Filled with wonder, he reported that "the whole island is a garden and all you can get from it is gold". In 1470, Christopher Columbus, come to buy sugar in Madeira, married the daughter of the captain-donatory of the island of Porto Santo.

After 1481, Portuguese discoveries increased: Diego Cam reached the mouth of the Congo and Bartolomeu Dias the Cape of Good Hope. At almost the same time, Columbus undertook his first voyage to the New World, financed by Ferdinand and Isabella of Spain. On his return, he put into Santa Maria in the Azores, where he was promptly arrested by a guard who took him for a pirate. He was released after a few days in captivity.

Madeira and the Azores became important advance bases for the Portuguese, and foreign merchants began to settle there. The islands' wealth attracted pirates, who made regular raids from 1497 onwards. In 1499, Vasco da Gama, who had just opened up the sea-route to India, made a long stop-over in Madeira then in the Azores where he buried his brother Paulo, who had died during the voyage. Portugal began to look westwards; Cabral landed in Brazil and began to explore it. A few decades later, when Portugal was at the height of its power and the world's leading maritime nation, prosperous pioneers returned from the New World, building baroque palaces and churches on the islands.

Spanish Rule

In 1580, upon the death of the last king of the Avis dynasty, Portugal, along with Madeira and the Azores, came under the domination of Spain. One of the great decisive battles in the conflict took place off São Miguel. Dom António, pretender to the throne of Portugal, was preparing his reconquest of the country at Terceira, which had remained loyal. Hoping for an alliance with Catherine de Medici, he offered her Brazil in return for her support, but she refused. The troops of Philip II of Spain landed at Angra do Heroismo. At first, the islanders managed to repel the attack, but two years later Dom António was defeated and forced to withdraw.

Under the 60 long years of Spanish rule, the islands became a port of call for Spanish galleons returning from America. Drawn by the fabulous treasures being transported, gangs of pirates and buccaneers patrolled the waters. A Spanish governor was sent to Madeira in 1582. The Fortaleza de São Tiago was built in Funchal, and the Pico de Castelo on Porto Santo. The timber trade was encouraged; many Spanish ships were built from Madeiran wood. In 1640, after 27 years of war, Portugal finally rose up and recovered its independence. The Duke of Bragança took the throne as João IV, but the country, impoverished by the conflict and supplanted by the Dutch in the East Indies, entered an era of decline.

Marc Michel

In these more peaceful times, Funchal's Fort of São Tiago houses the Museum of Contemporary Art.

Dalliance with England

Meanwhile, the Madeiran sugar trade began to suffer in face of competition from Brazil and the West Indies. The plantations were gradually replaced by more vineyards. João IV signed an agreement with British merchants, allowing them special concessions on exports, and in 1658, an association of merchants founded the British Factory on Madeira. Two years later, England decreed that only English ports could export wine to the colonies. In 1662, when Charles II of Great Britain married Catherine of Braganza, daughter of the king of Portugal, an alliance was formed between the two countries and Madeira was excluded from the ban the following year. As a result, the merchants of Madeira enjoyed a monopoly on wine exports to the New World and elsewhere.

During the War of the Spanish Succession, Portugal sided with Austria against France and Spain and escaped a new invasion thanks only to the British troops. In 1703, the Anglo-Portuguese alliance was strengthened by a commercial treaty. Many of His Majesty's ships called at Madeira, where they took on wine fortified with alcohol to help them withstand the rigours of a long voyage to the Orient. Unsold barrels were returned to Funchal, and it was discovered with some surprise that the hot temperatures and rolling movements of the ships had vastly improved the quality of the wine. It soon became famous throughout Europe.

From 1750 to 1777, Portugal was ruled by the iron hand of the all-powerful Marquis of Pombal, chief minister to the pleasure-loving king, José I. An enlightened despot and great reformer, notably of the education system, Pombal abolished slavery in Portugal in 1775. He was the first in the world to do so, though this reform completely disrupted the economy of Madeira and the Azores. He also expelled the Jesuits; they had established a college in Funchal in 1569 and owned many of Madeira's vineyards. In 1759 their estates were dismantled and sold off to more English wine merchants.

After the death of José I in 1777, Queen Maria dismissed the marquis, who was banished to his castle in Pombal, and set about undoing his achievements.

By the end of the 18th century, European medical circles had discovered the therapeutic value of Madeira's mild climate. Patients suffering from tuberculosis began to come in search of a remedy, or at least relief, in the warmth of the sun. The majority were from English families who had made money in the early days of the

Industrial Revolution. By now the British Factory was powerful enough to act as a colonial government for the British residents and helped to finance a British church, cemetery and hospital.

Napoleonic and Dynastic Wars

Queen Maria turned mad with grief after the death of her eldest son, her sister and other relatives from smallpox. Her son João acted as prince regent. Under Napoleon, the French attempted to break the Anglo-Portuguese alliance and close Portuguese ports to English ships, but French demands were refused. In 1807 Napoleon ordered General Junot to march on Lisbon, and the royal family, court and government fled to Brazil. British troops had been stationed on Madeira from 1801 to 1802, and they returned in 1807, this time staying for seven years. In 1808, the citizens of Porto locked up their French governor and reiterated their loyalty to the absent prince regent, sparking a movement that spread as far as the Algarve. From Brazil, João declared war on France. British troops, commanded by Sir Arthur Wellesley, the future Duke of Wellington, forced Junot to leave Portugal, and a council of regency was restored. In 1809 and 1810 Napoleon invaded the country again, and both times Wellington came to the rescue. The French were driven out of Portugal altogether in 1811; the country was ruled like a colony from Brazil and governed by the English General Beresford.

Maria died in 1816 and her son finally became King João VI. He returned to Portugal in 1821, after Beresford was overthrown by a military uprising. The following year he ratified a liberal constitution. Brazil, where his elder son ruled as Emperor Pedro I, became independent. At the death of João VI in 1826, a war of succession broke out between "absolutists", who favoured Miguel, younger son of the dead king, and "constitutionalists" who supported Maria, his granddaughter and daughter of Pedro I of Brazil, who had abdicated in her favour. A military expedition from the Azores participated in the rout of the absolutists in Porto.

Maria II acceded to the throne in 1834, but troubles continued to beset the country until 1853, when a system of suffrage based on taxation was introduced. In the Azores, the victory of the liberals introduced a period of expansion, synonymous with the development of the *quintas* and experiments with new crops: tobacco, tea, oranges and pineapples. Madeira, however, was hit by a series of disasters. The British Factory was forced to close down in 1838 after a decline in the wine

Blue memories of the good old days depicted in *azulejos*.

trade. Thousands of people died in a cholera epidemic in 1856, and the vineyards were wiped out by oïdium (powdery mildew) in 1852 and phylloxera in 1872. Then the remaining sugar plantations were hit by disease. Many poverty-stricken Madeirans emigrated to Portugal's other colonies and South America, and thousands more Portuguese followed them after the government declared itself bankrupt in 1892.

Nevertheless, the numbers of visitors to Madeira, many of them aristocrats and members of the European royal families, increased, gradually turning the island into a popular holiday destination. The majority of these early tourists, according to a now well-established tradition, were the British, followed by the Germans who built sumptuous *quintas* on the heights above Funchal. In 1895, Portugal accorded a limited autonomy to the islands.

Republic and Dictatorship

In the hope of resolving the economic crisis, Carlos I, reigning since 1889, appointed a strong-minded reformist, João Franco, as premier. In face of opposition, Franco dismissed the government and ruled by decree. Carlos and his heir, Luís Felipe, were assassinated in Lisbon in 1908. Franco vanished, and two years later, Carlos's younger son and successor, Manuel II, was forced into exile, which he lived out at Twickenham in England. The Republic was declared on October 5, 1910, ushering in another period of great instability.

During World War I, Portugal sided with the Allies. At England's request, Madeira confiscated all German property, and in retaliation, German submarines bombarded Funchal twice.

In 1926, a coup d'état brought to power a triumvirate headed by General Gomes da Costa. Two years later, he was succeeded by General Carmona, who brought in Dr Antonio Salazar de Oliveira as Finance Minister. At the head of an authoritarian government, Gomes da Costa set up the nationalist and corporatist "New State", but in 1932, Salazar took power. Despite countless strikes and several attempts to overthrow him, he held on to the reins until 1968 when he retired after a stroke (he died two years later).

Though Portugal was officially neutral during World War II, the Azores served as an Allied naval and air base in the name of an Anglo-Portuguese treaty of alliance dating from 1386. Two thousand British refugees from Gibraltar were evacuated to Madeira. The economy was badly affected by the war. Once peace had returned to Europe, a less elitist tourist industry began to develop on Madeira. Electricity was installed on Porto Santo only in 1954; the economy began to improve when a new crop was introduced in the 1960s, dwarf bananas. Subsidies were later introduced to counter this new threat to the wine trade. Airports were built in 1960 in Porto Santo and in 1964 in Madeira.

The Carnation Revolution

On April 25, 1974, the Portuguese army mutinied. In a few hours and without bloodshed, the Carnation Revolution put an end to 48 years of dictatorship. Acclaimed by the population, General Spinola set about establishing democracy. The secret police was disbanded, political prisoners freed and censorship suppressed. Spinola resigned three months later, leaving the field clear to the left. Amid chaos, the Socialists won the elections in 1975 and 1976. The Portuguese colonies in Africa obtained independence.

Autonomy

The Madeira Liberation Front (FLM) was created at the instigation of the great landowners, who were worried that the new government in Lisbon would expropriate their lands. The Azores Liberation Front (FLA) appeared at the same time but enjoyed little success among the islanders. To relieve pressure, the Portuguese Constitution made the islands into two autonomous regions in 1976, each with a local assembly, a regional government and a president.

With the entry of Portugal into the European Union in 1986, Madeira has greatly benefited from development aid. The standard of living has improved in spectacular fashion. New roads and bridges were built, along with schools, hospitals and training colleges. Hotels and resorts mushroomed, and the capital was spruced up for the millennium festivities. In 2000 the airport road was connected with the south coast highway, and a huge runway extension was opened. But Madeira is still planning for the future, and a Free Trade Zone has been developed near Caniçal on the eastern coast. This port and industrial zone has been granted tax-free status until 2011. The population remains stable at around 250,000, a third of whom live in Funchal.

Glittering between ocean and sky, Funchal is a spectacular sight.

Huber/Damm

MADEIRA AND PORTO SANTO

Madeira is a frivolous fragment of Portugal, like a vivid flower tossed from the shores of Europe into the ocean. Basking in a mild climate, it is a heady combination of exuberant vegetation, dramatic mountains and dizzying cliffs plunging sheer into the Atlantic. Its rather staid reputation is a thing of the past, as more and more young people come to enjoy the adventure sports on offer, round the coast or up on the mountain slopes. Offshore lies Porto Santo and its long beach of pale sand.

Funchal

The town stretches superbly round a wide bay where ocean-going liners drop anchor. Thousands of red-roofed houses cling to the steep slopes that were once carpeted in fennel, their gardens overflowing with greenery.

Almost half of Madeira's population lives in Funchal; a modern town geared for tourism, and bursting with life but still mindful of its colonial past. In the old town centre, fruit stalls line up beneath silk-cotton (kapok) trees, whose woolly buds burst open in spring, and jacarandas raining pink and blue petals. Parks and cobbled squares, discreet palaces and baroque churches recall the opulence of its Portuguese heritage. The centres of interest in Funchal are grouped reasonably closely together and can easily be visited on foot.

Seafront

Close to the old centre, **Avenida do Mar** (e das Comunidades Madeirenses) stretches round the bay from the harbour to the Old Town, carrying a steady procession of traffic. A quay juts out into the bay, separating the dark sand beach from the marina, where yachts and fishing boats tie up. All day long, residents and tourists alike flock down here to sit beneath the palm trees and sip their morning coffee, enjoy an afternoon drink or watch the night fall. This is the splendid setting of the firework display to herald the New Year, accompanied by a cacophony of ringing church bells answered by the sirens of the cruise ships out in the bay.

Against the pier, *The Vagrant*, a yacht built for the American millionaire Horace Vanderbilt and once owned by the Beatles, has been transformed into a seafood restaurant. Further east along the beach is a small stone column, the remains of the so-called **Banger's Tower** which once stood 30 m (100 ft) high. It was built in 1798 at great expense by a British merchant, John Banger, as a sort of crane to load goods off and on ships, and was demolished to make way for the promenade in 1939.

Alfândega Velha

On the far side of Avenida do Mar stands the old customs house, now the seat of the Parliament of Madeira. At the northern end, a fine Manueline doorway survived the 1748 earthquake, but the rest of the building has suffered unsightly reconstruction and modern extension.

Fortaleza e Palácio de São Lourenço

The first of Madeira's fortifications stands opposite the marina on the other side of the Avenida do Mar. It was built 1513, on the spot where João Gonçalves Zarco had landed a century earlier, but was still unfinished when a famous French pirate called Montluc pillaged the town in 1566. When the Spanish occupied the island they completed the construction and converted the fort into a palace. Today this is the official residence of the Minister of the Republic and sumptuously furnished; it is open for visits on Wednesday mornings and Friday afternoons (book at the main tourist office). When the minister is not in residence, you can visit the gardened courtyard; there are some old Portuguese *azulejos* in one corner.

The east wing of the fort is the headquarters of the military governor and is closed to the public.

Parque de Santa Catarina

Continuing westwards past the fort, Avenida do Mar merges into the Estrada da Pontinha below the Praça do Infante, a square reached by a flight of steps. Beyond it is Santa Catarina Park, landscaped over several levels. Pleasantly wooded and planted with flowers, it's a favourite spot with local families and courting couples, as well as children who love the playground at the top. The plain white **Chapel of Santa Catarina** was erected in the 16th century on the site of Madeira's first church, built in wood at the instigation of Zarco's wife in 1425. The chapel is closed to visitors, but from here you get a superb view over the sea and the town climbing up the mountainside. There's a small statue of Columbus nearby.

Quinta Vigia

On the north side of the park, the old *quinta* was variously the residence of Queen Adelaide, consort of King William IV of Great Britain, the Empress Elisabeth of Austria, and today, Madeira's governor. You can visit the 18th-century chapel, adorned with *azulejos* recounting the life of St Francis, and enjoy the sea view from the exotic gardens.

Hospício da Princesa

Founded by the Empress of Brazil in 1859, in memory of her daughter who died of tuberculosis, the hospice has a lovely shady garden that's open to the public.

Casino and Quinta Magnolia

The circular casino was designed by Brazil's foremost architect Oscar Niemeyer. From the terrace there's a superb view of the coast. Beyond, you can see the first grand hotels of Funchal—the Savoy, the Carlton, Reid's, lined up in a garland strung out over several kilometres. In between is Quinta Magnolia, formerly the home of the British Country Club and now a leisure complex where you can make use of the tennis courts, swimming pool and children's playground. The British Club houses a foreign-language lending library with a good collection of books in English.

Avenida Arriaga

This is the main thoroughfare of Funchal, planted with jacarandas and fetchingly paved with black

Reid's Hotel. Dominating the ocean to the west of Funchal, Reid's, set in a vast tropical park, was founded by the son of a Scottish crofter and inaugurated in 1891 (three years after Reid's death). Since then it has always been the unofficial headquarters of the members of British high society who took up residence in Madeira. An imposing parade of the rich and famous have patronized the hallowed walls of this illustrious example of Victorian architecture, from Elisabeth, Empress of Austria, who was one of its first guests, to George Bernard Shaw, Winston Churchill, Gregory Peck and Roger Moore. Churchill was particularly fond of the island, and the story is still told how he ordered a vintage Madeira dating from 1792—the oldest bottle in the hotel's cellars—and insisted on draping a napkin over his arm and pouring it himself. Nowadays, tea is still served on the terrace at five o'clock on the dot, as in the good old days, overlooking the gardens and the blue sea (correct attire required).

and white flagstones. The avenue runs parallel to the sea front on the north side of the Fortaleza de Saõ Lourenço, beginning at Praça do Infante.

Halfway along, on top of a fountain and supported by four statues of horses, is a model of a celestial sphere showing the movements of the stars in relation to the earth. It was the emblem of Henry the Navigator, whose statue stands close by. Note the attractive neo-Manueline façade of the Bank of Portugal.

Museu Barbeito Colecção Cristóvão Colombo

Walk east along the avenue and stop at No. 48, on the left-hand side just after Praça do Infante, at the Diogos Wine Shop. In the basement is a small museum with displays illustrating the visit of Columbus to Madeira. It also documents the history of the island by means of old portraits, ancient books and maps, historical prints, postcards and model ships.

Jardim de São Francisco

Also called the Municipal Gardens, these once belonged to an old convent. Ponds and fountains refresh the luxuriant tropical greenery, making a pleasing oasis in the busy centre of town.

To the north is a café and an open-air theatre, next to the old Scots Kirk, built of wood in 1861 and still serving the Presbyterian community.

Teatro Municipal Baltazar Diaz

On the south side of Avenida Arriaga, Funchal's main theatre was founded in 1888. Opera, ballet and musicals are staged in its sumptuous interior. Next door is the former Chamber of Commerce, clad in panels of *azulejos* depicting island life in the old days, showing the famous sledges used to slide down the cobbled streets of Funchal, a needlewoman, a fisherman, and so on. Part of the building is occupied by the Galerias São Lourenço, a shopping centre. Behind Rua Fontes is the north side of the São Lourenço fort.

Adegas de São Francisco

Past the Tourist Office at No. 18, you come to the São Francisco wine lodge, housed in part of a former Franciscan monastery in buildings clustered around a handsome cobbled courtyard. Here, the Madeira Wine Company runs an interesting cellar museum where you can see early wine presses, labels, old measuring tools, ancient vats of mahogany, oak and satinwood and other wine-making artefacts. The Company is a partnership of four of the island's biggest wine producers: Cossart Gordon, the oldest founded in 1745, Leacock (1760), Blandy (1811) and Miles (1878). It is worth joining a 90-minute guided tour (weekdays at 10.30 a.m. and 3.30 p.m., Saturdays at 11 a.m.) as you will enter rooms otherwise closed to the public. You'll see the great vats where the best vintages are left to mature for longer than the average person's lifetime, at temperatures above 30 °C (86°F). Some of the barrels can hold enough wine to fill 9,000 bottles. The visit includes a video presentation and culminates in a tasting of wines made from four grape varieties: Sercial (Riesling originally imported from the Rhineland), Bual (Boal from Burgundy), Malmsey (Malvasia from Crete) and Verdelho. There's nothing to stop you buying a bottle or two to take home—the oldest vintages on sale date from 1845!

Zarco Monument

Continuing eastwards along Avenida Arriaga you soon reach the junction with Avenida Zarco which leads down to the seafront on your right hand and up to Praça do Município on the left. In the middle of a roundabout stands a statue of Madeira's discoverer and founding father João Gonçalves Zarco, by local sculptor, Francisco Franco, and unveiled in 1934. Zarco was named governor of the island, an honour passed on to his descendants until the Spanish occupation.

Around the Cathedral

Avenida Arriaga ends opposite the red basalt portal of the **Sé**, Funchal's cathedral. Begun in 1485 and completed in 1514, it was financed by sugar, and was the first Portuguese cathedral built overseas. Its best feature is the magnificent panelled ceiling of gilded cedar wood encrusted with ivory, of Moorish inspiration. Typical of the Manueline period, when Portuguese architecture began to absorb exotic influences from its new discoveries, the ceiling is incontestably one of the finest examples of its kind—though you need a torch to see it properly as the building is very dark inside. In the two baroque side chapels, note the fine rose motif.

To the left of the choir, a door flanked by panels of *azulejos* tiles opens onto a charming little square where a **flower market** is held. The stall-holders wear traditional costume to sell their splendid bouquets of anthuriums and birds of paradise.

The streets north and south of the cathedral are mainly traffic-free. It is a good place for shopping for embroidery, jewellery and souvenirs, and there are several restaurants with pleasant outdoor terraces.

Museu Cidade do Açúcar

East of the Sé, in Praça do Colombo, the tiny Sugar Museum stands on the site of a building demolished in 1876, referred to as Columbus's House, though the explorer probably only stayed for a short while in the home of a Flemish sugar merchant, João Esmeraldo. The original well is displayed in the museum, with other artefacts retrieved from excavations of the building, maps and sugar-related objects such as moulds for forming sugar loaves and measuring instruments.

Praça do Município

The wide square, attractively paved in black and white, is a few blocks north of the cathedral. In the centre stands an obelisk topped by a celestial sphere and a cross. The north side of the square is formed by the buildings of the University of Madeira, a former Jesuit college (the Jesuits were banished from the island in 1760 by the Marquis of Pombal). The baroque **Igreja do Colégio**, built in the 17th century, has a black basalt and marble façade; inside are some lovely *azulejos*, a colourful painted ceiling and great gilded altarpieces.

The **Câmara Municipal**, or Town Hall, with a square tower, encloses the east end of the square. It is housed in the palace of the Count of Carvalhal, an 18th-century landowner. You can enter the central courtyard to admire its *azulejos*. Beyond are the law courts, Palácio de Justiça.

Museu de Arte Sacra

The white building on the south side of Praça do Município is the 18th-century Bishop's Palace, now the Museum of Religious Art. Temporary exhibitions are held on the ground floor, while upstairs is a collection of vestments and silver, sculpture and jewellery, and on the top floor, a magnificent hoard of Dutch and Flemish paintings, many of them commissioned by wealthy landowners directly from Flanders in the 15th and 16th centuries.

Instituto do Vinho de Madeira

Walk east from Praça do Município to reach Rua 5 de Outubro, which follows the bed of the Ribeira de Santa Luzia. To the north at No. 77, the grand yellow *quinta*, complete with watchtower, was the residence of the 19th-century English consul and wine merchant Henry Veitch. Today the home of the Madeira Wine Institute, it contains a small museum that deals rather didactically with wine production; you may see a cooper at work.

Around Rua da Carreira

Follow Rua Pestana west of Praça do Município and cross

Have some Madeira, m'dear!

Appreciated by European royalty, made into a famous sauce by the French, and particularly favoured by the British, Madeira is one of the world's most fabled fortified wines. Shakespeare must have been familiar with it, as he mentions it in *Henry IV (Part I)*, when a character ribs Falstaff about selling his soul to the devil "on Good Friday last, for a cup of Madeira and a cold capon's leg". In the early days of the Victorian era, English ladies perfumed their handkerchiefs with Madeira wine, while the Americans christened their frigate *USS Constitution* with a bottle. George Washington drank a pint every day. Today's vintners and merchants are mostly descendants of British families: Miles, Leacock, Cossart Gordon, Blandy, Shortridge, and so on.

Huber/Damm

over the end of Avenida Zarco to reach Rua da Carreira, where riderless horse races were held before cars were invented.

Museu Photographia Vicentes

At No. 43, around a pretty balconied patio, the Vicentes Photographic Studio—the oldest in Portugal—has been resuscitated to become a fascinating museum of photography. The founder, Vicente Gomas da Silva, began experimenting with daguerreotypes in the middle of the 19th century. The antique equipment he used to record the daily life of the islanders, landscapes and important events is displayed, and there are thousands of negatives and glass plates as well as sepia prints ranging from stiffly posed family portraits to holiday snaps of Winston Churchill.

São Pedro

Almost opposite the Vicentes Museum, Rua das Pretas climbs to a small square overlooked by the baroque parish church of São Pedro. The interior is decorated with rather plain *azulejos*, with an exuberant high altar of gilded wood and a trompe-l'œil ceiling.

Museu de História Natural e Aquário

Nearby, the Natural History (or Municipal) Museum stands on Rua de Mouraria in the Palácio de São Pedro, another residence of the Count of Carvalhal. It displays collections of butterflies, fossils, birds, native animals stuffed or reduced to skeletons, with a room devoted to sea creatures.

Casa Museu Frederico de Freitas

Continuing up the steep slope of the Calçada Santa Clara, stop at No. 7, just opposite the São Pedro Church, to visit this magnificent museum (known locally as the Casa da Calçada). The 18th-century mansion was the home of a lawyer who spent 30 years of his life travelling and compiling an eclectic collection ranging from oriental carpets and antique furniture to Chinese porcelain, North-African woodcarvings and English toby jugs! An annexe, the **Casa dos Azulejos**, displays on several floors Freitas's amazing collection of decorative tiles from Persia, Turkey, Syria, Madeira itself and even from the convent next door. The museum is closed Mondays.

Convento de Santa Clara

This working convent was founded at the end of the 15th century by one of Zarco's daughters. The original building was destroyed by a pirate attack in the 16th century and the nuns fled to Curral das Freiras in the centre of the island. It was rebuilt in the following century. You can visit the peaceful cloister, planted with orange trees, several chapels with azulejo-clad walls and painted doors and ceilings, and the superb church, resplendent in gold, glazed tiles and paintings. It is separated from the nuns' quarters by thick wooden grilles which permitted the girls to attend mass without any contact with the outside world. The rules were relaxed slightly in the 19th century when the nuns were allowed to sell homemade sweets to the congregation. Zarco's tomb is beneath the choir.

Quinta das Cruzes

Further uphill is the 17th-century Quinta das Cruzes, built on the site of the house where Zarco lived during the early years of the colony. Transformed into a museum, it has a collection of objects evoking the great Portuguese voyages of discovery: porcelain, two 16th-century Hispano-Arabic chests inlaid with gold and ivory, several great coffers, a superb Flemish altarpiece from the late-15th century and many pieces of furniture. These include local items made from planks from old sugar packing cases. There is also a palanquin, a popular method of transport for the fine ladies of Madeira in the 19th century.

The garden has become a repository for various architectural bits and pieces, including statues, tombstones and a Manueline window frame, that have been recuperated from some of the island's demolished buildings. They lie attractively scattered among tree-ferns and dragon trees, palms and orchids.

Fortaleza do Pico

The road winds up to the Pico Fort, also known as São João Baptista, guardian of Funchal and its bay at a height of 110 m (360 ft). Built during the Spanish occupation, between 1620 and 1640, it is now occupied by the Portuguese Navy.

British Cemetery

At the bottom of the hill, back on Rua da Carreira, is the British Cemetery, the final resting place of Protestants of many countries since 1887. Before then, they were not allowed in the Catholic cemeteries and had to be buried at sea.

English Church

Head back towards the centre, and turn up cobbled Rua do Quebra Costas on your left. A short walk uphill, at No. 18, is the domed neoclassical English Church, built in 1822. It was designed by the British Consul, Henry Veitch, and has neither spire nor arched windows; some claim that these were not allowed by the Catholic Church. In the garden is a bust of Philippa of Lancaster, daughter of John of Gaunt and wife of the Portuguese king, João I.

The British residents of Madeira and Protestant visitors now worship here and sing to the accompaniment of the huge organ, imported in parts from England and assembled on the spot.

Between the Rivers

Two rivers spread like the branches of the letter Y from the beach: Ribeira de Santa Luzia and Ribeira de João Gomes. Between the two is an area of shopping streets, hotels and offices. One of the busiest is Rua Dr Fernão Ornelas, stretching across from one river to the other.

Igreja do Carmo

From the top of Rua Ornelas, follow the arcades of Rua Cooperativa Agricula to Praça do Carmo, a spacious square nestling in the middle of a tangle of pedestrian streets. The Count of Carvalhal is buried in the 17th-century baroque church which eavesdrops on the chatter rising from the café terraces.

Museu Henrique e Francisco Franco

Northeast of here at 13, Rua de João de Deus is a small museum devoted to the two Franco brothers, the painter Henrique and sculptor Francisco (known for his monument to Zarco, p. 19). Francisco was commissioned by Salazar to portray many of Portugal's great heroes; the plaster moulds are displayed in the museum, along with a bronze bust of Salazar. Henrique's bold, colourful paintings depict scenes of Madeiran life.

IBTAM

On the west bank of Ribeira de João Gomes, at 44, Rua do Visconde de Anadia, the Instituto de Bordados, Tapeçarias e Embutidos do Madeira, set up in 1978, displays some of the finest pieces of embroidery and handicrafts by the island women and perpetuates the needleworking traditions by providing training. On the upper floor is a museum displaying intricate exhibits ranging from handkerchiefs to bed linen, along with black-and-white photographs taken by Vicente Gomes da Silva in the early 20th century. In the main hallway, the huge tapestry of a local landscape, *Allegory of Madeira,* is made up of 7 million stitches and took three girls three years to complete.

Old Town

East of Ribeira de João Gomes is the friendly Zona Velha, where spruced-up fishermen's houses—some of them dating back to Funchal's foundation—line the cobbled streets. Among them are countless bars, fish restaurants and taverns where you're likely to hear the mournful wails of the *fado* pouring into the street in the later hours of the evening.

istockphoto.com/Hills

The busiest market. Built in the 1930s, the **Mercado dos Lavradores** sells fish, fruit, vegetables, flowers, local crafts, clothes and pet birds. It is one of the most colourful markets in Europe, at its liveliest on Saturday mornings.

Mercado dos Lavradores

Set around a central courtyard, the covered market is a large, attractive yellow building with a cladding of *azulejos*. From the arcaded tiers of the upper floors you can look down on the stalls, where shoppers gossip with gusto among the trays of beetroot and figs, mangoes and avocados. Submerged in a haze of luscious orchids, lascivious anthuriums and perky strelitzias, the flower-sellers are decked out in traditional costumes. One side of the building on the ground floor is devoted entirely to fish and seafood, the counters heaving with glistening tentacles and thick juicy tuna steaks, crabs and winkles and rows of steely black scabbard fish with fine hair-like tails.

Museu de Electricidade

The name may not turn you on, but it is worth popping into this museum to get a new angle on island life from the electrical point of view. It is housed in the former Central Power Station, down the road from the central market on the way to the sea front, and traces the story of lighting from olive oil lamps through water-powered generators to modern technology and alternative energy.

Fortaleza de São Tiago

Continuing east along the seafront, past the cable car station for Monte, you will soon reach the ochre-walled fortress of St James, built by the Spanish in 1614. During the Napoleonic Wars, 3,500 British troops were stationed here. You can walk round the ramparts, browse around the unprepossessing collection of maps and weapons in the Military Room, or head for the Museu de Arte Contemporanea in the former military governor's house. Most of the works on display are by mainland Portuguese, though there are some paintings by Madeiran artist Eduardo de Freitas on the bottom floor. Unless you're a great fan of modern art you may find the displays rather disquieting, if not thought-provoking.

Praia da Barreirinha

At the foot of the fortress, painted boats quietly await their next departure, while people of all ages paddle in the seawater pool of the Lido, a low-key cluster of gym, café and changing rooms, with a pebble beach close by.

Santa Maria Maior

The 18th-century baroque white and dark grey church was built on the site of a chapel that commemorated the plague of 1538. On the façade is a statue of the Virgin and the arms of the town. Every May 1, a procession is held here in honour of the plague victims.

Follow Rua de Santa Maria back to the centre—it is one of Funchal's oldest streets, with some of the Zona Velha's best-known restaurants and some fascinating little shops.

Strelitzias on the lookout, above the formal beds of the Jardim Botânico.

Bertie Schrafner

Around Funchal

On the steep slopes around Funchal are some of the island's most spectacular sites, all within a radius of 10 km (6 miles) and easily reachable by bus or taxi. Further inland, this earthly paradise hides a heart of stone. Often veiled in cloud, the craggy volcanic peaks beckon more and more hikers to explore the island's natural wonders.

Gardens

Several *quintas* in the leafy suburbs a few kilometres to the northeast of the city have opened their splendid gardens to the public. They can all be combined in one trip, with a walk back down to Funchal afterwards.

Jardim Botânico

You can potter around the lovely gardens of the Quinta do Bom Successo for hours without being disturbed. The estate belonged to the Reids, and the grounds have been open to the public since 1960. Pride of place is given to indigenous species from Madeira and Porto Santo, or plants from other Portuguese islands—the Azores and Cape Verde, but there are flowers and trees from all over the world. Best are the orchid garden, the medicinal herbs, the colourful bedding plants and the collection of cacti and succulents in all shapes and sizes. These are near the **Museu de História Natural**, occupying the old house. Its exhibits are not exactly thrilling, mostly stuffed or fossilized. A café provides refreshments and a good view of Funchal; you can also look around the **Loiro Parque** (Parrot Park), full of parakeets, cockatoos, peacocks and macaws, cohabiting happily with geese, ducks and a giant tortoise.

Jardim Orquídea

At 37, Rua Pita da Silva, a short walk below the Parrot Park, this orchid garden set up by an Austrian specializes in raising baby plants for export to Europe in little glass jars. Whatever season you visit, several of the 5,000 plants of more than 300 species cultivated in the nurseries will be in bloom. In the laboratory you can see every stage of the cultivation procedure, from sterilization of the seeds to the glorious flower. To show how orchids grow in natural surroundings, the owners have created a miniature jungle complete with birds and fish.

Quinta da Boa Vista

The former British Consul Cecil Garton and his wife run their estate's fine orchid collection, set out in rows of pots and including many rare species. It is on Rua da Boa Vista, downhill from the terminus of the No. 32 bus line.

Once you have had an eye-full of the glorious flowers, enjoy the "boa vista" from the lawn, where tables and chairs are set out and tea sometimes served.

Quinta do Palheiro Ferreiro

Out on the road to Camacha, a turning leads to the so-called Blacksmith's Estate, also known as Blandy's, which boasts the most beautiful of all the gardens on this flower-blessed island (open weekdays only). The estate was founded by the Count of Carvalhal but has belonged to the Blandy family since 1884—the first Blandy to arrive on Madeira was John, aged 23, a quartermaster in General Beresford's army. The Count of Carvalhal set out formal gardens in his 12 ha (30 acres) of land, with ornamental ponds, geometrical flower beds and topiary, and planted English trees—beech, oak and chestnut—which thrived in the cooler atmosphere at this altitude (600 m, 1,970 ft). In their turn, the Blandys added plants from all around the world. At the end of an avenue of camellias, which billow into white, pink and red blossom from December to April, the garden is revealed in all its splendour—more than 3,000 species of plants forming a lush carpet. A path leads down into the Inferno, a ravine where the giant ferns have been left to grow into jungle.

East of the gardens is the gorgeous 18-hole golf course, **Balancal Palheira Golf** and a hotel where you can have drinks on the lawn.

Camacha

About 14 km (9 miles) northeast of Funchal, Camacha, set in the midst of willow plantations, is Madeira's wickerwork capital, a trade that has been plied in earnest here since 1850. On one side of the large cobbled main square, Largo da Achada, a little sign boasts that this was the site of the first football match ever played in Portugal (1875).

Dominating the south side of the square, the large white O Relógio building, named for its clocktower, embraces a café, a restaurant and a huge handicrafts centre. In the shop here you can buy anything imaginable in wicker, from a place mat to an elephant, and you can watch the craftsmen toiling away in the downstairs workshop. Also on sale are ceramics from the mainland, *azulejos*, wines, liqueurs and other souvenirs.

Monte

The glass bubble of a cable car floats you up from Funchal seafront over the rooftops of the Zona Velha to Monte in 10 minutes. The hilltop town sits at 550 m (1,800 ft) north of the city, looking out over the bay. Thanks to its cool climate and wonderful views, Monte became a favourite health resort in the 19th century, playing host to wealthy islanders and sickly members of European royalty and aristocracy, come to heal their ailments and indispositions in the sun.

Nossa Senhora do Monte

Karl I, the last of the Habsburg emperors, and his wife Zita of Bourbon-Parma came to live his exile in Madeira at the Quinta Gordon in Monte. The emperor's health was delicate and he died of pneumonia aged only 35. He is buried in a side chapel of this twin-towered church, which stands at the top of a winding flight of 74 stone steps that begins behind a fountain on Monte's main square. The first church here was built in 1470 by one of the first children born on the island, Adam Gonçalves Ferreira. (His twin sister was called Eve.) It was destroyed in an earthquake and another, baroque church built in the early 19th century.

However, the church's main claim to fame is not its imperial connections but a small statue of the Virgin on the central altar. Panels of *azulejos* on the façade recount how the statue was discovered in the 15th century by a shepherdess in the village of Terreiro da Luta north of Monte. It is worshipped in particular on the Feast of the Assumption in August, when devout Catholics climb the steps to the church on their knees.

Monte Palace Tropical Garden

Back at the main square, follow Caminho das Baboas to reach the entrance of Madeira's most fantastic park. This Portuguese-Japanese Garden of Eden was the brainchild of an 18th-century tobacco magnate, José Rodrigues Berardo and contains not only an abundance of exotic plants but also fountains, statues, koi fish ponds, Japanese bridges, stone lanterns, a dragon, a Manueline

The floweriest gardens. In the **Jardim Botânico**, clinging to the terraces above Funchal, succulents and tropical plants, rare trees and exotic flowers grow side by side. Even higher, thousands of plants thrive in the gardens of **Quinta do Palheiro Ferreiro**, but the most spectacular of all are the camellias.

www.madeiratourism.org/DRTM

Marc Michel

Today, only tourists make use of the quaint *carros de cesto*.

door from the 18th century, 40 *azulejo* panels depicting great moments in Portuguese history, and 166 glazed panels illustrating what is termed "The Adventure of the Portuguese in Japan"—social, commercial and cultural links between the two countries.

The **Monte Palace Museum** in the grounds has a permanent display of about 1,000 semi-precious stones ("Mother Nature's Secrets") and two floors devoted to a large collection of contemporary stone sculpture from Zimbabwe ("African Passion").

In the café beyond the lake you can drink a glass of Madeira, included in the park entrance ticket.

Terreiro da Luta

A short detour of 3 km (2 miles) north takes you to the spot where the shepherdess discovered the famous statue of the Virgin. A monument was erected there in 1927 to commemorate the end of World War I. When German submarines attacked Funchal in 1916, the Madeirans prayed to the Virgin of Monte and promised to build a statue of the Virgin if the war was stopped. The anchor chains you see at the base of the monument came from the French ship that was destroyed in the German offensive.

Toboggan Ride

The early residents of Madeira invented a quick and easy way to carry their produce downhill to market and back up again—in *carros de cesto*, large baskets on wooden runners pulled by horses and bullocks. In the 19th century someone had the bright idea of adapting them so that two drivers could steer the sledges and transport the landowners down from their *quintas*. This caught on as a novelty with tourists.

Clad in white trousers, white shirt and straw boaters, the drivers oil the wooden runners with greasy rags so they slide easily down the road, and keep the contraption under control by means of ropes, braking with the rubber soles of their goatskin boots. The ride generally stops in Livramento where taxis wait to take passengers back to Funchal. It is possible to negotiate a ride all the way down to town but this is not recommended because of the traffic.

Pico do Arieiro

The road heading inland after Terreiro da Luta heads directly to Pico do Arieiro, the island's third-highest peak, alt. 1,818 m (5,965 ft). Just after Terreiro da Luta, a narrow paved track on the left takes you to Pico Alto, alt. 1,129 m (3,704 ft), where there is a bewitching view over Funchal. Back on the main road, you will soon reach the Poiso pass, where a fork off to the west climbs even higher, skirting vertiginously deep ravines, and the landscape gradually gets more barren. The road ends in a lunar landscape of weatherworn rocks and basalt columns of lava rising from the red earth.

Steps lead up from the car park to the summit. If the day is clear, the view is stunning: in the southwest dips the hollow of Curral das Freiras, to the northwest is the crest of Pico Ruivo, Madeira's highest point at 1,862 m (6,109 ft). The serried ranks of mountains crowd all around, and far in the east is the eastern tip of the island at São Lourenço. A rough 10-km (6-mile) track winds up to Pico Ruivo, a three-hour hike away. Many ramblers spend a night in Pico do Arieiro's small *pousada*. You can walk down in 10 minutes to the *miradouro* at Juncal for a totally different view.

istockphoto.com/Greve

Levadas. Water channels hollowed out of the ground or carved in the rock, tunneling beneath the mountains or striding over valleys on aqueducts, the *levadas* of Madeira form a unique irrigation system. The network was begun by the first settlers and developed over the centuries; today it extends for 2,150 km (1,335 miles), conveying rainwater from the central mountains down to the cultivated plots of land. Reaching every corner of the island, the *levadas*, paralleled by gently sloping paths, provide a system that could not have been better designed for exploring the interior. There are plenty of locally published guidebooks mapping and rating the walks; you should never attempt these alone and it is recommended that you hire a guide.

From the viewing platform of Pico do Arieiro you can contemplate the craggy peak of Pico Ruivo above the mist.

istockphoto.com/Bogaerts

Balcões

From the Poiso pass, which forms a veritable climate barrier between the south and the cloudy north of the island, you can continue northwards instead of turning off to Pico do Arieiro, dropping down to Ribeiro Frio and its trout farm in a gardened setting (the fish feature on the menu of the local restaurant). At the exit of the village, a pleasant path alongside the Levada do Furado climbs up to the *miradouro* of Balcões, providing one of the island's most stunning views. The series of wooden balconies hangs over a vast rocky bowl, and on a fine clear day you can see all of Madeira's main peaks: Pico do Juncal and Arieiro, and further north Pico das Torres and Ruivo. Another path leads east, still following the Levada do Furado, reaching the **Portela** viewpoint in about three hours.

Curral das Freiras

Heading west of Funchal to the suburb of São Martinho, you'll see the towering Pico dos Barcelos, alt. 355 m (1,165 ft), where the inevitable *miradouro* affords a fine view over Funchal and its bay. From there, the road climbs steeply through eucalyptus woods up to Curral das Freiras. This valley used to be so remote and difficult to reach that nuns from the Convento de Santa Clara in Funchal, who used it for farming, sought refuge there during a pirate attack in 1566. They founded the village that became known as "Valley of the Nuns".

As you near the end of the 22-km (13-mile) road, take a detour to Eira do Serrado. A short walk away from the hotel, restaurant and shopping complex is another breathtaking *miradouro* on a rocky ledge over 400 m (1,300 ft) above the horseshoe-shaped valley of the Ribeira dos Socorridos, its steep flanks carved into terraces, with the white flower-clad houses of the village nestling down at the bottom. All around, a regiment of cloud-wisped peaks stands guard. When you have drunk in as much as you can of the view, walk down to the village along a winding cobbled

The loftiest views. From sheer cliffs to sharp peaks, Madeira's landscapes are nothing short of majestic. At **Cabo Girão**, the cliffs make a vertical plunge of 580 m (1,903 ft), the European record! The panoramas are countless, but some are more heart-stopping than others: the wooden balconies of **Balcões** look out onto the island's highest summits, and **Eira do Serrado** gives an eagle's-eye view of Curral das Freiras from an altitude of over 1,000 m (3,500 ft).

An imperial wine. As prisoner of the British, a rather disconsolate Napoleon made an involuntary stay on Madeira on his way to his final place of exile, the island of St Helena. To give him some solace, the British consul sent him a barrel of good Madeira wine. However, the deposed emperor never got a chance to enjoy it: he was suffering agony with stomach pains, and his gaolers either feared the wine was poisoned or just wanted to torment him, and the barrel remained untouched. Years after Napoleon's death, the unpaid bill came to light. The new British consul demanded the return of the barrel. It was eventually returned to the Blandy Company in 1840. The wine was bottled and marketed under the label "Battle of Waterloo"!

track leading from the car park (it takes about 90 minutes), or continue along the road, through tunnels and round hairpin bends.

The villagers live mainly from agriculture, basketmaking and tourism. They also produce a cherry liqueur, *jinja*. The church built by the nuns was replaced by a new one, Nossa Senhora do Livramento, in the 19th century; it contains attractive *azulejos* and a stained-glass window.

Câmara de Lobos

On the most densely populated side of the island, the lovely little fishing port of Câmara de Lobos takes its name from the flocks of monk seals resting on the rocks when Zarco landed after his second voyage in 1420. The village huddles in a cove between the sea and rocks but is slowly spreading up among the terraces that cover every cultivable plot of land. Coming from Funchal, just before you reach the village, a viewing platform affords a splendid panorama of the cluster of houses, boats swaying in the wind, fish drying on racks, the coastline, and the cliff of Cabo Girão rising in the distance. This was a favourite spot of Winston Churchill, who would set up his easel here and record the view in watercolours.

Brightly painted fishing boats jostle for space in the harbour, near the black shingle beach. Look inside the fishermen's chapel, **Nossa Senhora da Conceiçao**, where the inside walls are adorned with paintings depicting shipwrecks and people drowning.

A concrete building at the harbourside is the site of the fish market at 7 a.m. The most highly prized catch here is *espada*, the black scabbardfish gleaming like a cutlass blade.

At the exit of the village, a road leads off to the right to the *mira-*

douro at Pico da Torre. The 360° view pans around the port and the sea, along the coast and up over the banana plantations and the mountains.

Estreito de Câmara de Lobos

The road to Cabo Girão snakes up through the vineyards to this quiet village in the middle of one of Madeira's main wine-producing areas. In early September, during the Wine Festival, the harvest is celebrated here with processions in traditional costume, folk dancing and grape-treading.

The road continues up the mountain slope to the hamlet of Jardim da Serra and the pink *quinta* of the well-meaning British Consul who had a barrel of Madeira delivered to Napoleon during his stopover on the island.

From the end of the road, where there's a stunning view over the hamlet of Curral das Freiras wedged into the mountains, a hiking trail leads towards the heart of the island. Another track from Jardim da Serra winds through the vineyards to the *miradouro* of Boca dos Namorados, with a westerly view over Ribeira dos Socorridos.

Claude Hervé-Bazin

All dressed up for the Wine Festival in Estreito de Câmara de Lobos.

Cabo Girão

From Estreito de Câmara de Lobos, the road turns back down to the coast, reaching the sea near the pine- and eucalyptus-clad headland of Cabo Girão (Cape Turnaround, named by Zarco who got this far on his first exploration of the coast then turned back to Funchal). From the lookout platform, built out over the sea (with railings you can cling to), there's a dizzying view down to the foot of the cliffs 580 m (1,900 ft) below. The panorama sweeps from the Bay of Funchal in the east to Ponta do Sol in the west. This is a popular stop for coach tours and can get crowded. A strip of land around the base of the cliffs is under cultivation.

Terraced slopes and rocky terrain—an engineer's dream, or nightmare?

Marc Michel

Around Madeira

The island has to be discovered at a gentle pace. Covered in dips and folds like a rumpled blanket hemmed by a rugged rampart of cliffs, its thick velvet pile of greenery culminating in eucalyptus and pine, it is not the ideal terrain for building wide, straight roads. The island is fairly small, 22 km (14 miles) wide and 57 km (35 miles) from end to end, and despite the construction of modern, fast highways and tunnels, you will only average 30 to 40 kph (18 to 25 mph) on the twisting roads further from Funchal.

East Coast

The south coast highway takes you from Funchal to the airport in 20 to 30 minutes. The road actually passes under the extended runways—long enough for jumbo jets to land—propped up on stilts over the sea.

Caniço

Just east of the capital, Caniço and Caniço de Baixa (Lower Caniço) are built up with modern hotel complexes and villas, mostly inhabited by the German community, and there's a good selection of restaurants. Off the beach at Lido Galo Mar is the underwater marine park of the **Reserva Natural Parcial do Garajau**; you can hire snorkelling or scuba diving equipment to explore the depths.

Santa Cruz

Behind its palm-fringed seafront promenade, Santa Cruz clusters around a 16th-century church with Manueline features. Near the leafy main square, the 19th-century courthouse is an attractive building in grey and white, now housing the police headquarters and government offices. The pebble beach has a play area for children; behind it there's a small covered market. Continuing east from the beach you reach the Lido, with a seawater pool. You can have a picnic in the public gardens and look out at the view of the Ilhas Desertas (see p. 38).

Machico

Madeira's second city was its first settlement, where Robert Machin and his mistress Anne d'Arfet are said to have been shipwrecked, and where João Gonçalves Zarco landed in 1419. No one knows for sure whether he named the place after a tombstone he found inscribed "Robert Machin", or if it was derived from Monchique, his birthplace in Portugal, or perhaps the name of the boatswain of his caravel.

A 10-minute drive north of the airport, Machico lies at the mouth of the river of the same name, at the heart of a wide bay. As you approach, you'll catch glimpses of the houses piled at the bottom of the valley, with boats pulled up onto dry land above the pebble beach.

On the north side of the main square, Largo Dr António Jardim d'Oliveira, stands the church of **Nossa Senhora da Conceiçao**, built in 1499 in the late 15th century when Machico was the island's capital. The arched Manueline side door has three marble columns with carved capitals, a gift from Manuel I who also donated the statue of the Virgin inside. The interior is baroque, with a painted ceiling.

East of the square, walk past the town hall and cross the bridge over the river to the Banda de Alén, the old fishermen's quarter. Here you will find the **Capela dos Milagres** (Chapel of Miracles), said to have been built on the site where Anne d'Arfet and Robert Machin were buried. A former chapel on this spot was destroyed by flood in 1803, but a wooden crucifix was swept out to sea and rescued by a passing ship. Another chapel was built to house this "miraculous" cross in 1815.

istockphoto.com/Ariza

Wildlife havens. The three **Ilhas Desertas**, 20 km (12 miles) south-east of Funchal, are indeed deserted, apart from the odd scientist or two. There is no regular ferry service, though boat trips are arranged from the marina in Funchal. Sports fishermen come from Madeira in pursuit of tuna and wahoo. Since 1990, the islands have been the protected domain of the rare monk seal, turtles, dolphins and seabirds such as the Madeiran shearwater. Deserta Grande, the largest of the three islands, 12 km (7 miles) long and 1 km (just over half a mile) wide, was inhabited by a few settlers until the early 19th century when their homes were flattened by a tornado. They led a meagre existence gathering a orchella weeds *(Roccella tinctoria)*, yielding a red or purple dye (orchil or cudbear) used for dyeing silk and wool.

Much further away, halfway to the Canary Islands, the three **Selvagens** (Savage Islands) were declared a nature reserve in 1971 when they became the property of the Portuguese government (until then they were owned by a rich banking family, the Rocha Machados). As breeding grounds for shearwaters, they are surveyed by sentries who make sure that no one steps ashore.

Each October 8, a torch-lit procession is held to celebrate its recovery, and the next day is a public holiday.

Down by the seafront is the old market building, transformed into a restaurant, and the yellow-painted **Forte do Amparo**, built in 1706 as protection against pirates and now housing the tourist office. In front of it, a row of cannon point out to sea, and to the east is the new market. Further along the road you come to boatyards then the **Forte de São João Baptista**, just above the spot where Vaz Teixeira and Gonçalves Zarco disembarked on July 2, 1419.

The town beach stretches west of Forte do Amparo, mostly pebbles but with a sandy strip at low tide. Beyond it is the palm-lined **Passeio Marítimo**, ending near the Capela de São Roque; usually it is locked so you can't see the lovely *azulejos* inside.

A road strikes inland from Machico, climbing in a series of bends through eucalyptus forest. It passes the Santo da Serra golf course and culminates at the **Portela** lookout, 669 m (2,195 ft), before descending to Porto da Cruz and Faial on the north coast.

Pico do Facho

Continuing along the coast after Machico, you can take a detour to this summit, at 322 m (1,056 ft),

istockphoto.com/Lindner

Crimson volcanic rocks on the island's rugged coastline.

named after the beacon that used to be lit here. From the top you get a birds'-eye view over the airport on one side and the São Lourenço peninsula on the other.

Caniçal

The road to Caniçal passes through a tunnel bored beneath Pico do Facho. The local government decided to turn the town into a free trade zone, which explains the warehouses and factories at one end of the beach. Otherwise this former whaling port is quite attractive (John Huston filmed part of *Moby Dick* here). Now the offshore waters are part of a marine reserve, and its small museum, Museu da Baleia, is dedicated to whale conservation. The history of whaling is documented by objects made of whale bone and teeth, model boats, an authentic whaler, old photographs, and a video on marine animal protection.

Ponta de São Lourenço

In the east, Madeira fizzles out in a long, straggly peninsula, windswept and deserted. Past a small wind farm (Parque Eólico), steps lead down the cliff to Madeira's one and only sandy beach at Prainha—dark grey-brown sand. If you follow the rough path on your left, you'll reach a good viewpoint over the north side of the peninsula and a handful of islands lashed by the waves.

The road ends just before the deep curve of Baia de Abra. From the car park, a footpath winds high over the cliffs to the tip of the headland through the Parque Natural de Ponte de São Lourenço. Beyond are two islets, Ilhéu da Cevada and Ilhéu do Farol, topped by a lighthouse. The walk takes about three hours, there and back. In fine weather, you can see Porto Santo on the horizon.

The West

From Ribeira Brava to Santa Maria Madalena, the west coast is dotted with sleepy villages, some facing out to the sea, others turned towards the terraced fields.

Ribeira Brava

Sheltered at the foot of a gorge where the "angry river" flows, this busy resort is full of cafés, restaurants and shops. Sugar cane was grown here, and at the town hall, which used to be the home of a sugar merchant, you can see odd bits of mill machinery lying around in the grounds. Facing the public gardens, the 16th-century **Igreja de São Bento** with its chequered roof has a Manueline font and pulpit carved with animals and plants. The **Ethnographical Museum** occupies a pink 16th-century town house that used to be a rum distillery. The modest displays give some insight into local crafts and trades.

Boca da Encumeada

A road inland from Ribeira Brava follows the river past terraced slopes to the mountain village of Serra de Agua, the site of one of the island's *pousadas*.

Continue climbing as far as the Encumeada pass, at 1,077 m (3,304 ft). From here, surrounded by sharp ridges and canyon-like valleys, and if the wind sweeps away the clouds, you can look back over Ribeira Brava and forwards over São Vicente on the north coast, to the horizon where ocean blends with sky.

From the pass, several tracks lead into the heart of the central mountains. One goes to Curral das Freiras and Jardin da Serra, another winds up hill and down vale to Pico Ruivo, at one point passing through a tunnel carved out from the rock in the early 19th century for the pleasure of British ramblers.

Paúl da Serra

The road leading west from the Encumeada pass takes you through a craggy landscape and a series of tunnels to Bica de Cana and on to the bleak moorland of the Serra plateau, a wide expanse of flat land. Far from the constraints of civilization, herds of wild horses run free. Every June, the island's shepherds meet up here for their annual Festa da Tosquia sheep-shearing festival.

From the beautiful valley of **Rabaçal**, further west, an hour-long hike along a *levada* ends at the 25 Fontes waterfall. If you're short of time, take the turn-off to the right along the way for an easier *levada* ramble to the Risco falls, some 100 m (320 ft) high. To the north stretches the Fanal plain, where flocks of sheep graze around the roots of gnarled, mist-swathed trees. Another *levada* walk from Rabaçal, over lonely moorland, ends at the statue of Cristo Rei, Christ the King, a miniature version of the statue in Rio de Janeiro.

www.madeiratourism.org/DRTM

The Festa da Tosquia is held amid much merrymaking.

Ponta do Sol

Back on the coast road, the next town after Ribeira Brava is sun-splashed Ponta do Sol, amidst banana plantations. The 18th-century baroque church, **Nossa Senhora da Luz**, has a painted wooden ceiling depicting biblical scenes and beautiful *azulejos*. Up in one of the steep cobbled streets is the home of the grandparents of American writer John Dos Passos, pointed out by a plaque on the wall. It is now a library.

Madalena do Mar

Wedged between banana plantations and the sea, this village is said to have been founded in 1414 by a defeated king of Poland, Wladislaw II, who escaped to the island and was granted lands by Zarco. Known as Henry the German, he married a local woman and was drowned at sea on his way to Lisbon. His body was recovered and is buried in the village's Igreja de Santa Caterina.

Calheta

With time in store, you can enjoy a drive along the old road from Ponta do Sol, bypassing Madalena do Mar and winding up and down the mountainsides, through several picturesque villages.

The quick road follows the coast, and you will reach Calheta in 10 minutes or so. It's a pretty old town; the first governors were Zarco's children. You can visit a working rum distillery, **Engheno da Calheta**, with the usual chance to taste and buy at the end of the free tour. Above the distillery, the unadorned church, **Igreja Matriz**, has a splendidly riotous ebony and silver tabernacle inside, a gift of Manuel I.

Inland, to the north, Estreito da Calheta is worth a visit for the **Capelo dos Reis Magos** and its 16th-century Flemish altar carving of the Adoration of the Magi.

Centro das Artes, Casa das Mudas

High on a promontory west of Calheta, at Ponta do Este, this daring new museum and modern art centre was designed by a local architect, Paulo David. In perfect harmony with the landscape, sea and sky, the flat and angular museum provides a spectacular showcase for Madeiran artists.

Western Tip

The villages are fewer and further between after Calheta as the road plunges more deeply into sweet-smelling forests of pine and eucalyptus. A turn-off takes you to **Jardim do Mar**, a neat and pretty fishing village with narrow alleys lined by flower-laden houses. High on a rock ledge are several viewpoints overlooking the rocky beach and thrashing waves; to the west you can see the next village of **Paúl do Mar** beneath beetling cliffs. At low tide, it's possible to walk there along the coastal path, but the sea does not stay out long enough for you to return.

Inland, **Prazeres** is the start of the pleasant Levada Nova walk through wooded countryside to **Ponta do Pargo** (Dolphin Point), at the western tip of the island, stopping at a red-hatted lighthouse. The view sweeps over the cliffs dropping sheer into the sea.

The next stretch of the road winds through forest in one of the last populated areas of Madeira. Shortly after Santa Maria Madalena, it drops down towards Porto Moniz, affording views of the village, the coast and plantations.

North Coast

The north coast is the most rugged, the wildest and wettest part of the island, but probably also the most beautiful. The road passes through one tunnel after another, the end of each one opening onto dizzying panoramas of untamed, green cliffs with tiny villages tucked beneath their toes.

Porto Moniz

Named after a former governor, Francisco Moniz, this lively town once depended on whaling and farming on the steep terraces for its revenues, but has now turned to tourism. The buildings of old and new towns cluster on a tongue of land, sheltered from the elements by the offshore Ilhéu Mole. Stretching up the slopes is a patchwork of fields, some hardly bigger than an outspread sheet, embroidered round the edges with fences of heather broom or drystone walls, protecting the crops from the wind.

On either side of the harbour, bobbing with colourful fishing boats, are two sets of natural sea pools that have formed in the black volcanic rock. As they are fairly shallow, the water warms up in summer, to the delight of islanders and tourists alike.

A few kilometres out of town, take the side road to Lamaceiros and the start of the **Levada da Central da Ribeira da Janela**, a 2.5-hour walk through ancient laurisilva (laurel) forest, protected by UNESCO. Ribeira da Janela village is delicately poised between two vertical rock walls at the entrance to a deep, wild and uninhabited valley.

istockphoto.com/Abreu

Deep within the ancient and mossy laurisilva forest.

Seixal

Another 6 km (4 miles) along the coast road, Seixal clings to a spit of land framed in green cliffs that are cultivated to the very limits. Some of the terraced vineyards seem suspended in space, high above the ocean. Others, the most overgrown, have been abandoned, as they could only be reached by climbing a rope. The island's best grapes are grown here—malvasia, a speciality of the north coast.

Down in the village, a few fishing boats lie at anchor in the harbour. To put to sea, the fishermen have to use a crane.

Between Seixal and São Vicente, waterfalls cascade over the road into the sea. You can see them close to from the *miradouro* at Véu da Nova, a short drive out of town.

São Vicente

At the junction with the trans-island road to Ribeira Brava, São Vicente is a well-developed resort, with its hotels set apart from the picturesque old town. Overlooking a palm-shaded cobbled square, the 17th-century baroque church has a painting of St Vincent on the ceiling and fine *azulejos* on the walls.

Outside town, the **Grutas de São Vicente** are underground caves carved out of the volcanic rock, underlined by streams and rock pools. The tour of the tunnels includes commentary and piped music.

Ponta Delgada

The coast road snakes from one valley to the next over some 45 km (28 miles), passing between terraces of vines and densely overgrown mountains. First, it passes Ponta Delgada, spread out over a *fajã*, a cultivated strip of low-lying land. In the heart of the village, on the seafront, the **Igreja do Bom Jesus** boasts a prized relic: a wooden crucifix that was washed ashore in a chest in the 15th century. The church built to house it burnt down in 1908 but the cross was merely charred. The present church was erected in 1919. Nearby, the modern **Casa de Cultura** hosts temporary exhibitions of arts and science. A path leads to the **Piscina** sea pools.

At the village exit, look back at the lovely view of the church, white houses and rocky coast.

Boaventura

The single-track road, carved out of the cliff, winds inland to the agricultural settlement of Boaventura overlooking the entrance to the Ribeira do Pôrco. At the bottom of the valley—a huge circle of mountains scarred with steep terraces—lies the village of **Fajã do Penedo**. The road twists back towards the coast and Arco de São Jorge, suspended between green cliffs, vines and ocean. A little way out of the village, there is a magnificent panorama from the viewing platform of **Cabanas**, a tourist resort of round white huts inspired by Zulu design: in front of you, cliffs plunge down for 600 m (1,970 ft).

Santana

Once past São Jorge and its lighthouse (affording splendid views of the coast), you reach Santana, known for its traditional A-frame houses, the floor of the bedroom beneath the eaves forming the crossbar of the A. The thatched roofs almost reach the ground, and inside the rooms are just high enough for a person to stand. Many have been turned into cowsheds with corrugated iron roofs, but there are still a few thatched ones to be seen.

Santana is the site of the popular **Madeira Theme Park**, with fun-filled attractions based on local traditions, and radical sports like bungee jumping.

About a kilometre below Santana, the **Rocha do Navio Teleférico** is a cable car plunging down the cliff to a cultivated *fajã* on the shore, where there's a café, a stony beach and good views.

Queimadas and the mountains

From Santana, a pot-holed road climbs through luxuriant laurisilva forest up to the Casa das Queimadas, a thatched government-run rest house with picnic tables outside. From here, follow the *levada* path through woodland and hydrangeas to the **Caldeirão Verde**, a hollow of moss-covered rocks, with a waterfall and small lake nearby. The path is steep and narrow in places, and winds through four low tunnels; it takes about two hours. An hour further along the path, for experienced hikers only, is another waterfall at **Caldeirão do Inferno**.

A shorter path from the Casa das Queimadas goes to **Pico das Pedras**, a pleasant picnic spot. You can get to the same place by road from Santana to Achada do Teixeira, an easier option.

From the car park at the rest house of Achada do Teixeira, a fairly gentle paved path takes you in an hour or so to the summit of **Pico Ruivo**. The panorama at the top takes in all the central mountains, including Pico do Areiro, which can be reached by a spectacular but difficult two-hour hike.

Claude Hervé-Bazin

The fishermen can work quite close to shore.

Faial

East of Santana, Faial is a small agricultural village spreading over the hillside around a church adorned with *azulejos*. From the square outside you have an excellent view of Penha de Águia, a sheer-sided cube-shaped mountain 590 m (1,935 ft) high. You can drive back to Funchal via Ribeiro Frio and the Poiso pass.

Porto da Cruz

This lively fishing village affords stunning views of the coast from its harbour. At the west end of the promenade is a large seawater pool. The village is the start of a scenic if sometimes precipitous coastal path via Lorana to Machico. It takes from three to four hours, one way.

istockphoto.com/Annoyingbartender

www.madeiratourism.org/Fernandes

Huber/Gräfenhain

Porto Santo

Porto Santo, 75 km (46 miles) north-east of Madeira, is totally different from its sister island. It is quite small, only 14 km (9 miles long) and 5 km (3 miles) wide, and has been little developed. There is a ban on new building on the north coast.

The landscape is barren, swept and eroded by salt-laden winds that turn the sails of windmills. The eastern end of the island is dominated by conical mountain peaks: Pico do Castelo, 437 m (1,433 ft), Pico do Facho, 516 m (1,692 ft) and Pico Branco, 450 m (1,476 ft), but the rest is largely flat. Its great asset is the wide golden beach underlining the south coast, stretching 9 km (5.5 miles) from Portela to Miradouro das Flores.

Vila Baleira

The island capital on the south coast is a picturesque collection of 16th- and 17th-century buildings with terracotta roofs. Palm-shaded Avenida Infante Dom Henrique leads to the main square, **Largo do Pelhourinho**. On one side is the Town Hall, its façade adorned with coats of

Porto Santo has the advantage of a long, curving beach of golden sand, with a backdrop of conical peaks.

arms, and on another the 17th-century Igreja de Nossa Senhora de Piedade, which replaced the original church that was destroyed by pirates. There are panels of *azulejos* inside and out.

In 1479 Christopher Columbus married Filipa Moniz, the daughter of the island's first governor, Bartolomeu Perestrelo. The couple met after a church service in Machico. A house in Vila Baleira (signposted next to the church) is designated as their home, and was turned into the **Casa Museu Cristóvão Colombo** in 1992, to celebrate the 500th anniversary of the discovery of America. The marriage did not last long, because Filipa died in childbirth in 1484. The museum displays portraits, maps and ship models related to Columbus and his voyages, as well as household items donated by islanders and objects retrieved from a shipwreck.

South of Largo do Pelourinho, an avenue of palms leads to the **Infante Gardens**, with a statue of Christopher Columbus and other sculptures commemorating the Voyages of Discovery and the Boatmen of Porto Santo. The water from the drinking fountain near the playground is rich in calcium and said to be good for the kidneys—or give you eternal youth.

The best, sandiest part of the town beach is west of the jetty.

Around the Island

Two- to four-hour sightseeing tours are organized in an open-topped bus or jeep, or you can rent a car, a scooter or a bicycle to explore the island at your leisure. An unhurried way of visiting the immediate surroundings of Vila Baleira is in a *carriola*, an old-fashioned trap pulled by a pony. You can also book a boat trip to the small outlying islands, or take to your legs and hike around the mountains to Terra Chã, the northernmost tip of the island.

Northwest of Vila Baleira, **Quinta das Palmeiras** is a botanical garden forming a pleasant oasis in one of the island's most arid areas. Amid superbly landscaped gardens of vines, fruit trees and exotic flowers, toucans, parrots and other birds sing and whistle from their cages.

On summer weekends, Madeirans come in their hundreds to enjoy Porto Santo's beach. The sand is said to have therapeutic qualities, and you will see people buried in it up to their necks. The turquoise waters are an enticing invitation to go diving and windsurfing. The further west you go, the wider and more beautiful is the beach.

In a dramatic setting, **Porto Santo Golfe** in the west part of the island was designed by Severiano Ballesteros to blend into the landscape of dunes and basalt cliffs.

Stairway to heaven, or the church of Nossa Senhora da Paz in Vila Franca do Campo.

Huber/Gräfenhain

THE AZORES

High cliffs battered by the waves, creeks and crater lakes, geysers and hot springs: the Azores give a general impression of nature in the raw. The climate is mild, the vegetation profuse. From São Miguel, the showcase of the archipelago, to tiny Corvo, each of these nine islands has its own personality; it would be a pity not to see them all. They are divided into three groups: São Miguel and Santa Maria in the east; Terceira, Graciosa, São Jorge, Pico and Faial in the centre; Flores and Corvo to the west.

São Miguel and Santa Maria

Formed from two volcanic massifs, spangled with spectacular crater lakes, São Miguel is 62 km (38 miles) long and 16 km (10 miles) across at its widest point. The largest island of the archipelago has amassed all the principal economic activities, giving rise to its nickname of "little Japan". Half of the population is concentrated here, nudging the density up to 400 inhabitants per sq km of cultivable land. Also known as the Green Island for its patchwork of terraced plantations and lush pastures, São Miguel is so fertile that some years there are no less than four harvests. Bananas, oranges, sugar cane, tea, tobacco, grapes and cereals are cultivated, along with pineapples, matured under glass and exported to North America. From end to end, it is one immense garden. The 150,000 inhabitants are mostly descended from Portuguese and Breton colonists. Proud of their small paradise, they can tell you without batting an eyelid that earthquakes on São Miguel are less violent than on the neighbouring islands.

Ponta Delgada

The capital of the Azores since 1546, Ponta Delgada hems a wide bay on the south coast, at the foot of round-topped hills. The city is dynamic and overcrowded but has not lost its colonial charm. Its streets are narrow, its roads and squares paved with geometric patterns in black and white. Baroque churches, attractive old houses with red-tiled roofs, wrought-iron balconies and flower-filled gardens all add to its appeal.

Sea Front

Lined with banks, travel agencies and hotels—not forgetting the Tourist Office—broad Avenida Infante D. Henrique runs the length of the sea front, protected by a large pier where merchant ships and ferries tie up. Almost all the sights of interest are close to this avenue.

At the east end of the avenue is a large swimming pool, the marina and the fishermen's district, watched over by the church of their patron saint, São Pedro.

The fort of **São Brás**, at the western end, was built in the 16th century. It is occupied by the Portuguese navy today, so you can't visit.

Praça 5 de Outubro

Near the São Brás fort, this shady square is bordered by the city's two main historic sites. On the western side stands the baroque church of **São José**, built between the 16th and 18th centuries. The lower part of the choir is entirely covered in panels of *azulejos*, while the upper part, up to the painted ceiling, is made of carved and gilded wood. The side chapel is also decorated with tiles.

On the north side of the square, the convent of **Nossa Senhora da Esperança** is famed for its richly decorated statue of Santo Cristo dos Milagres (Christ of Miracles), a gift of Pope Paul III in 1530. Every year on the fifth Sunday after Easter, the townsfolk follow the statue, carried in reverent procession through the streets carpeted in petals. This is a working convent; you can enter the cloister by a small door on Avenida Roberto Ivens. The walls of the little church housing the statue are covered in fine panels of *azulejos* illustrating scenes from the Bible. A museum of religion occupies an adjoining room.

Largo de Matriz

Halfway along Avenida Infante D. Henrique, this airy arcaded square is the heart of the city. On the north side stands La Matriz, the parish church of **São Sebastião**, patron saint of the town. The church was first built between 1533 and 1545 to a rather plain design, and it was modified later. The main façade and door, in distinct Manueline style, were brought from Portugal and rebuilt here stone by stone; however, the interior is typically baroque. Note the richly carved cedarwood framework of the choir and the high altar in white stucco, covered in thousands of different motifs.

The church is surrounded by Ponta Delgada's main shopping streets, where you'll find jewellers, souvenir shops and plenty of cafés where you can sit and watch all the bustle.

Museu Carlos Machado

A few streets to the north, the museum occupies the buildings of the 16th-century convent and church of São André. It is divided into several sections enclosing a courtyard: ethnography, religious art, natural history, the development of *azulejos*, and so on.

A short walk west along Dr. G. P. Falcão Street is the church of **Todos os Santos** (All Saints), next to a small park. It was built in baroque style in the 17th century on the site of an older Jesuit college and has magnificent carvings and ceramic tiles in the interior. The college building houses the city library and archives.

Walking east from the museum you reach the **covered market**, under a vast modern roof. Apart from fruit and vegetable stalls, there are several craft outlets.

Around the Island

Winding roads, some paved, some asphalted, encircle the island. You will discover a rugged volcanic landscape of crater lakes and dizzying cliffs, dotted with quiet rural villages, in total contrast to Ponta Delgada.

Sete Cidades

From the capital and the south coast, several minor roads weave between green pastures and pine forests over the slopes of an extinct volcano up to the Sete Cidades crater in the northwestern corner of the island. Ever since the Azores appeared on the map, this fascinating place has inspired many a legend. Some say that one of the seven cities of Atlantis was located here before being engulfed during the cataclysm that wiped out the entire continent. Others claim that all seven of the mighty cities of Atlantis disappeared into the depths of the crater. Another version speaks of seven cities founded by seven bishops fleeing Moorish invaders long before the official discovery of the Azores in the 15th century.

Billowing banks of hydrangeas surround the **Visto do Rei** (King's Belvedere), looking out over the enormous caldera forming a gash in the earth. With a width of 5 km (3 miles) and 12 km (7.5 miles) in circumference, it encloses two lakes. **Lagoa Azul**, the larger of the two, is sapphire blue, separated by a narrow strip of land from **Lagoa Verde**, emerald green in colour. The difference in hue can only be observed in fine weather. A romantic legend attributes the phenomenon to a shepherd and a princess whose love was doomed

Huber/Gräfenhain

istockphoto.com/De Nijs

and whose abundant tears created the two distinct bodies of water.

A road descends in hairpin bends from the rim of the crater, with another splendid view from **Serrados das Freiras**. Once it reaches the level of the lakes, the road threads between them to arrive at the village of Sete Cidades, surrounded by green pastures. You can also walk all round the crater, following a well-worn track. The best time to tackle this is early morning, before the clouds gather round the summit.

North and East Coasts

The view from Ponta do Escalvado, high above the Atlantic breakers, is a vast panorama of the Mosteiros coast, famed for its vineyards. A short distance along the coast, the village of **Bretanha** was founded by Breton immigrants, as its name suggests. Continuing eastwards, you will notice tobacco leaves hung out to dry, first at the entrance to Santo António and again before **Ribeira Grande**. The latter is the second-largest town of the island, founded in 1507 and set in a geothermic area. There are several good views over the north coast,

Taking the milk to be collected. | São Miguel's orange groves were destroyed by disease and replaced by tobacco and other crops in the 19th century.

including one from Santa Iria. At the end of a turn-off, **Porto Formoso** has a small, grey sandy beach, Praia dos Moinhos.

Further on, just after São Brás, the slopes are covered with tea bushes. **Chá Gorreana** is the only tea plantation in Europe and was founded in 1883: it can be visited daily from May to September.

After the turn-off for Furnas, the road winds slowly along at some distance from the coast as far as **Nordeste**, a charming white village at the eastern end of the island. The wildest and arguably the most beautiful part of the island, between Nordeste and Povoação, is called **Decima Ilha** (tenth island) by the locals because it seems like another world. Steep cliffs plunge down into the sea, rushing streams have carved deep gorges in the rock, the luxuriant vegetation is festooned with a profusion of wild flowers, all to be admired from viewing platforms all along the road, landscaped like gardens.

Lagoa do Fogo

A road from Ribeira Grande or Lagoa on the south coast winds across fields and through woods of Japanese cedar to Lagoa do Fogo (Lake of Fire), a shimmering crater lake set in the heart of the island and framed by green mountains. A footpath leads from the edge of the caldera, where the view is superb, down to the water's edge. Part of the shore is rimmed with sand.

Vale das Furnas

In the southeast of the island, this valley is one of the highlights of any visit to São Miguel. At the bottom of an ancient crater, the village is reputed for its 22 thermal springs and their therapeutic properties with regard to rheumatism and digestive problems. Outside the village in the Provoção direction is an area of *caldeiras* (mudpots) and vents hissing sulphurous steam, where people come for picnics at weekends. The cooks set off at 4 a.m. to prepare their local speciality, *cozido das furnas*. Before daybreak, the ingredients of a tasty stew of meat and vegetables are packed into clay pots and lowered into deep holes excavated in the steaming earth; by lunchtime it is ready to eat. *Cozido das furnas* is also prepared at a similar picnic area further on at Lagoa das Furnas, pitted with bubbling mudpots and fumaroles.

Terra Nostra

Outside the village on the road to Ponta Delgada, the botanical garden is the perfect place for walking off the after-effects of too much *cozido das furnas*. It was designed by an American at the end of the 19th century, and surrounds an old mansion. There are several pools, including one where you can bathe in warm, ferruginous water (which leaves rust-coloured stains on light bathing costumes). The garden contains ancient trees from the four corners of the earth, including magnificent cedars, as well as palms, bamboos and tree ferns.

Miradouro de Pico do Ferro

From this lookout point, a 20-minute drive from Furnas, the view sweeps over one of the island's most beautiful landscapes: Lagoa das Furnas and the mountains encircling the town.

South Coast

Ribeira Quente, at the end of a dead-end road, has one of the most attractive beaches of São Miguel.

On your way back to Ponta Delgada you'll pass through the island's first capital, **Vila Franca do Campo**. It's worth looking round to discover its unusual square flanked by three churches. Nossa Senhora da Estrela (1517) is notable for its canvases by Flemish painters and a collection of figurines made from rice flour.

Beneath an old fort is a small port where boats tie up side by side; you can see an island, Ilhéu de Vila Franca just offshore. In the summer, locals come down here at weekends armed with large nets to sweep the waves in search of a seaweed that provides fabric dyes. An impressive flight of steps leads up to the Marian sanctuary of **Nossa Senhora da Paz** high above the village; from the top there's a spectacular view of the whole region. Further west is the large and attractive brown sand beach of Praia.

Caloura has a very pretty sheltered beach and a small fishing port complete with diving centre. There are several lookout points in the region, including Agua de Pau, affording splendid views over the south coast.

Before returning to Ponta Delgada, the road passes through **Lagoa** and then **São Roque**, whose beach, Praia das Milicias, gets very busy at the weekend. You'll see lots of greenhouses in this area, inside them are rows of pineapple plants.

Santa Maria

The first of the Azores to be discovered and the closest to Europe, Santa Maria has 6,000 inhabitants in its 97 sq km (37 sq miles). It was settled by poor peasants from the Algarve, and its houses have the tall white chimneys typical of that region. Until the 19th century, many of the islanders lived from harvesting *Roccella tinctoria*, a lichen used to obtain a purple dye. The American army built an airport in 1944

Pineapples. The pineapple was brought to the island in the 19th century as an ornamental plant for the gardens of the *quintas*. From 1850, they began to be grown commercially under glass. By 1910, a million fruit were being produced. Today, more than 7,000 family-run hothouses scattered throughout the Azores deliver over 3 million pineapples annually to the European and North-American markets.

istockphoto.com/De Nijs

which became a transatlantic stopover after the war.

Vila do Porto

On the south coast, the island's chief town, Vila do Porto is set on a hillside between the deep channels of the Ribeira Grande and Ribeira Sancho. The principal church, **Nossa Senhora da Assunção**, has carefully preserved the iron rods used by pirates in 1676 to beat the population into submission.

Around the Island

Santa Maria is proud of its tidy villages, its many churches and chapels of Manueline and baroque influence, and its lovely beaches. In the northeast, the most rugged area of the island, the bay of **São Lourenço** forms a vast hollow carpeted with plantations in terraces—one of the most striking landscapes in all the Azores. Facing the tiny Ilhéu do Romeiro is a pretty little stretch of pale sand; the beach is popular with divers.

A road full of hairpin bends winds up to the summit of **Pico Alto**, the island's highest point. From here and from many points along the north coast, you get impressive views of Santa Maria and its rugged coastline.

In the island's northwest corner stands the small white chapel of **Anjos**, the oldest in the Azores, where Christopher Columbus and his crew prayed on their return from the first voyage to the Americas. The high altar came from the caravel of Gonçalo Velho, who discovered the archipelago.

The bucolic landscape of Terceira is ideal for healthy exercise.

istockphoto.com/Vale Sousa

Terceira, Graciosa and São Jorge

Oval in shape, Terceira was the third of the Azores to be discovered, hence its name. By sheer coincidence, it is also the third in surface area, 403 sq km (156 sq miles), and in its position in the archipelago, counting from east to west. But in population, it takes second place, with 55,000 inhabitants.

Terceira was conceded to Jacome de Bruges in 1450 and was the first island to experience Flemish colonization. It is also considered a courageous island, as indicated by the name of its main town, Angra do Heroísmo (Bay of Heroism), taking part in all the region's battles. It was the last Portuguese bastion to resist the Spanish invaders at the end of the 16th century and the stronghold of the liberals in 1830. Away from the coast, the landscape is volcanic, dotted with dairy farms and patches of forest, criss-crossed by hedges of hydrangeas.

The Espírito Santo festivals are celebrated with special fervour in Terceira, culminating in the famous *touradas a corda* when bulls are released into the streets.

The best festivals. The countless festas mix sacred and profane. On Madeira, the **Flower Festival** heralds the arrival of spring. In the Azores, the processions of the **Santo Cristo dos Milagres** in Ponta Delgada and then the **Espírito Santo** bring out all the inhabitants onto streets strewn with flower petals. The grape harvest is celebrated in autumn everywhere that grapes are grown. On Madeira, the **Wine Festival** goes back to the very roots of tradition.

Angra do Heroísmo

The first settlement of the Azores to be elevated to the status of a town in 1534, Angra do Heroísmo owes its name to one of the strangest battles in the history of Portugal, which took place on July 25, 1581 at Salga, southeast of the town. In 1580, when Philip II of Spain seized the throne of Portugal, the inhabitants rose up in protest. Philip sent 10 of his ships to quell the uprising. After bombarding Angra, the sailors tried to find a place to land and to take on water near Salga. An ingenious idea came to the Portuguese resistants, and very soon more than a thousand cows (as many as enemy soldiers), maddened by the noise of the cannon, were stampeding in the bay. The Spanish were put to flight and many were drowned. Among the survivors was a one-armed man aged about 30, only recently released from the prisons of the

Barbary pirates—Miguel de Cervantes. The city was finally conquered in 1583, and until the middle of the 17th century it became a favourite port of call for ships returning from the East or the New World.

Monte Brasil

Though it suffered many times at the hands of pirates, Angra do Heroísmo managed to preserve the unique architecture of its golden age, which has been listed as a World Heritage Site by UNESCO. For your first view of the town, with its white houses and sea of red-tiled roofs, go to the top of Monte Brasil, an ancient volcano that rose from the seabed before the rest of the island was appeared. It forms a spit of land overlooking Angra from the south. The towers and

Impérios and emperors. More than all the other islands of the Azores, Terceira boasts a remarkable number of *impérios*, tiny chapels dedicated to the Holy Spirit. Most of them are painted in bright colours and maintained by a religious brotherhood. Each year at Whitsuntide, there are important celebrations involving colourful processions and mingling religious devotion with more profane high spirits. A bull or a calf, patiently garlanded with ribbons and purified with holy water, is sacrificed for the occasion and then shared out among the inhabitants at a village feast. Some of the villagers, chosen according to a practice in vogue in Europe during the Middle Ages, are charged with the duty of placing offerings of food for the poor in the *impérios*. At the same time, an "emperor", chosen in the old days from among the needy, but nowadays one of the children, is crowned.

istockphoto.com/Jacobs

walls of the imposing fortress of **São João Baptista** frame the base of the peninsula. It was built just after the Spanish conquest by order of Philip II and is still occupied by the army today.

Around Town

Next to the town hall, on pretty Praça Velha, horse-drawn carriages wait to take you on a leisurely tour. Nearby is the 16th-century cathedral, **Santíssimo Salvador da Sé**, twin bell-towers, their roofs clad in blue and white ceramic tiles. Inside, the ceiling is of carved cedar wood and the altar in wrought silver. The 17th-century **Palácio Bettencourt** is now the municipal library; its interior walls are adorned with magnificent panels of *azulejos*.

To the west, at the end of Rua do Barcelos, is the **Convent and Church of São Gonçalo**, the city's oldest convent and largest church, richly decorated with gilt carved altar panels, carved choir stalls and wall panels of *azulejos*.

North of Praça Velha, adjoining the Palace of the Captain-Generals, the church of **Nossa Senhora do Carmo** is known for its rich collection of 17th-century Dutch pottery.

The **Museum of Angra do Heroísmo**, just above a pleasant public garden, is housed in the former Convent of São Francisco. Its collections include arms, ceramics and musical instruments, and there's a large ethnographical section.

Returning to the centre, you can also visit the baroque 16th-century church of **Nossa Senhora da Conceição** and the 18th-century church of **Misericórdia**, with carvings and *azulejos*.

West Coast

Though most of the island's sights of interest are concentrated in Angra, the hinterland is very pleasant to explore. A road circles the coast in some 70 km (43 miles). Driving clockwise from Angra, the first place you come to is **Cinco Ribeiras**, badly shaken by an earthquake in the summer of 1998, then **Doze Ribeiras**. Shortly after Serreta, take the narrow dead-end road to reach a lighthouse and **Ponta do Queimado**, the most westerly point of the island. The coast road passes through a magnificent eucalyptus forest before reaching the lookout point at **Ponta do Raminho**, where you get a good view of fields clutching the top of the cliffs.

Biscoitos

Since the 15th century, the highly reputed 14° proof *vinho verdelho* has been produced from the vines of Biscoitos on the north coast. Protected from the ocean spray by stone walls, the vines creep along the ground, sending their roots down among the volcanic rocks. An instructive little Wine Museum, founded by the Brum family of Flemish extraction—the name is a corruption of De Bruyn—will teach you everything about the production of this wine, which once filled the holds of caravels on their way to India and Brazil. If you visit at the end of August or in early September, you may be at the right time to see how the grapes are pressed.

Before you leave the village, take a dip in the natural swimming pools formed in an old lava flow at Ponta dos Biscoitos.

East

Lajes has grown up around the airport and an American base. It was here that a meeting took place in 1971 between the French President Georges Pompidou who flew in on Concord, and the American President Richard Nixon, and here that in March 2002 President Bush and prime ministers Blair and Aznar met for their pre-Iraq summit, at a similar distance from Washington, London and Madrid.

A short distance further along the coast there's a good beach of brown sand at **Praia da Vitoria**, one of the few beaches on Terceira. As you make your way back to Angra, near **Porto Judeu** you'll see a multitude of tiny vineyards facing the Ilheu das Cabras, a good diving site.

Centre

The interior features ancient volcanic cones, old lava flows overgrown by pastureland and forests of eucalyptus and Japanese cedar. In the west is the huge **Guilherme Moniz caldera**, with a circumference of 15 km (9 miles). You can see a basalt grotto at **Algar do Carvão** and fumaroles nearby at **Furnas do Enxofre**.

Graciosa

Northwest of Terceira, the small and flattish island of Graciosa, with an area of 62 sq km (24 sq miles), lives far aloof from the madding modern way of life. Its windmill-scattered landscape presents an image of bucolic serenity. The 5,000 inhabitants are mainly clustered in Santa Cruz da Graciosa in the northeast. The 16th-century Igreja Matriz surveys the town's main square, planted with monkey puzzle trees. There is an interesting little ethnographical museum which is largely concerned with the winemaking tradition of the island: it produces an excellent white wine called Terra do Conde.

In the southeast, you might like to visit the **Furnas do Enxofre**, a cavern with an amazing black subterranean lake of hot sulphurous water down at the bottom, some 80 m (260 ft) deep. The best time to see it is at midday, when the sun is high enough to light up the interior. Fishing and diving facilities are also available on Graciosa.

São Jorge

Wild and steep, 56 km (35 miles) long by 8 km (5 miles) wide, São Jorge is basically a thin string of volcanoes rising to 1,053 m (3,455 ft) at its highest point, the **Pico da Esperança**. Forests of pine, beech, chestnut and laurel grow on the upper slopes, above meadows grazed by cows. The roads wind between hedges of hydrangea above black cliffs battered by the ocean waves—particularly impressive on the north coast. Here and there, lookout points reveal villages clinging to the water's edge or hanging precariously over precipices. Strips of low-lying fertile land, *fajãs*, are completely covered with crops, vines and bananas, using every last scrap of precious growing-space. At **Norte Pequeno** there's a splendid view over fields rising in tiers, bounded by a network of low stone walls. Elsewhere in other *fajãs*, beds of shellfish and crustaceans are rare resources for the island's 10,000 inhabitants, along with a famous cheese exported as far as Portugal.

istockphoto.com/Vale Sousa

hemis.fr/Barbier

Huber/Gräfenhain

Hydrangeas are the emblematic flower of the Azores. | Fajã do Ouvidor on São Jorge. | Island cheeses ripening slowly.

In their meadows hemmed by lava walls, the cows of Pico will greet you with a friendly "Muu".

istockphoto.com/Hafenmann

Pico

Pico is the second-largest isle of the Azores, and with only 15,000 inhabitants one of the least densely populated. It is named after the majestic volcanic cone, Pico Alto, that dominates the island; at 2,351 m (7,713 ft) it is the highest point in the whole of Portugal.

Arid, probably more Mediterranean in character than its neighbours, it is also one of the poorest islands of the Azores. The inhabitants long maintained the ancient tradition of harpoon-fishing on the high seas for sperm whales, from whalers or simple rowing boats, *botes*. Vines are planted along the shores in little hollows dug out of the lava crust with pickaxes, and protected from the spray-laden winds by black lava walls tracing square patterns. They produce one of the most appreciated of Azorean wines, a *vinho verdelho* with a slightly sulphurous taste. Traditional festivals, such as Bom Jesus at São Mateus or the Whalers' Festival at Lajes do Pico, are the occasion for the hardy population to demonstrate their willingness to enjoy life despite their sometimes harsh existence.

Lajes do Pico

Pico has three *concelhos*, or centres of local government. Lajes do Pico, on the south coast, is one of them. Its **Ecomuseum of Whaling** is not to be missed. It houses a fascinating collection of souvenirs: objects in whalebone, carved whale teeth, an authentic whaling boat, and so on. Excursions by Zodiac are organized from the small port, to observe the dolphins and whales that frequent the surrounding seas.

Around the Island

To the east, the road encircling the island overlooks the ocean, offering wonderful views of the coast. From Terras, there's a panorama of the village of **Cruz Santa Barbara**, the fields outlined by low walls, the lava coastline and the cliffs at the eastern tip.

Spectacular volcanic landscapes. Thrust forth from the ocean deep, the Azores still bear the scars of their difficult delivery. If **Pico**, with its almost perfect cone, is unsurpassed in majesty, **Capelhinos** can claim to be the youngest volcano. Close by is the yawning basin of the **Caldeira**, which gave birth to Faial. But the two most beautiful legacies of the Azorean volcanoes are to be found on São Miguel, where the lakes of **Sete Cidades** and **Lagoa do Fogo** gleam in the depths of ancient craters, amid a profusion of hydrangeas.

istockphoto.com/Mrfotos

Lava stones are used for building; here a wine cellar.

Many of the village houses were built in volcanic stone in the 17th and 18th centuries. Beyond the eastern point, the north coast is spectacular, plunging in places almost vertically into the sea. A landscape of forest and terraced fields of corn unfurls, with ancient lava flows *(mistérios)* and villages huddled around white churches. A short distance from the coast you can make out the long backbone of São Jorge island. Near the airport, the road branches off to **Arcos do Cachorro**, where the waves crash through arches worn through the lava. Their name comes from one eroded rock that resembles the muzzle of a small dog.

At the western tip of the island, the *Cruzeiro do Canal* plies back and forth in any kind of weather from the port of Madalena to Horta on the island of Faial. The boat sticks so closely to its timetable that the vineyard workers can set their watches by it. Beyond, the gentle contours of the countryside are quilted with a patchwork of vines.

Volcanoes

From São Roque, Madalena or Lajes, several roads climb to the mountains, where the ever-present Pico looms over the landscape. It is formed of **Pico Alto**, a circular crater, and **Pico Piquinho**, a volcanic cone inside it, 70 m (230 ft) high, that lets off occasional wisps of smoke. One road crosses the island from east to west, past hilly pastures, skirting ancient volcanic cones shrouded in cloud, revealing views of north and south coasts in turn. At the foot of Pico, a turn-off takes you to the start of a path that leads up to the summit. The panorama from the top, crowned with snow in midwinter, takes in the whole central group of islands. Firemen are posted at the beginning of the path; they keep the volcano under close observation 24 hours a day. If you want to climb up, you have to register with them when you set off and again when you return. Good walkers can make the ascent in three hours and the descent in two. Some like to spend the night at the top in order to watch the rising sun: adequate clothing is a must as the temperature is very cold in both summer and winter.

WHALING

In the Azores, the whaling tradition (illegal since 1986) is believed to go back to the 16th century, when Portuguese fishermen called in at the islands on their way to the banks of Newfoundland. It became a veritable industry with the arrival of American whalers at the end of the 18th century. In 1768 alone, 200 boats were prowling the waters around the islands. In the 19th century, local crews were taken on, establishing links between the islands and New England, where some of the expatriate population live today.

The whalers sought precious ambergris, a substance similar to cholesterol formed around the beaks of squid that collected in the large intestine of old male sperm whales. Ambergris was used in the fragrance industry for fixing perfumes. The yield per whale was 10 to 20 kg, and up to the 1980s its market value was around £2,500 per kg. The sperm whale also produced spermaceti, a white waxy substance contained in large quantities in the creature's head, and believed to have the biological function of melting or solidifying to compensate during dives for the high pressures experienced at depth. It was used in perfumery and cosmetics, and also in candles. Today's cosmetic industry has replaced it with jojoba oil, of similar chemical composition.

Rare today, the sperm whale commonly measures 15 to 20 m in length (50 to 65 ft) or more, and can weigh up to 70 tons. King of the cetaceans, it belongs to the *Odontoceti* type, with a row of large, cone-shaped teeth in the lower jaw and an S-shaped blowhole on the left side of its head. It swallows fish, squid and marine mammals whole, whereas the *Mysticeti*, or baleen whale, with two blowholes, has no teeth and sieves fish and tiny crustaceans through a comb-like structure. The sperm whale holds the world record for diving, both for duration of dive (up to 2 hours) and for depth—2,000–3,000 m (65,000–98,000 ft).

hemis.fr/Giraudou

Horta's Café Sport has long been famed as a meeting place for yachtsmen.

Huber / Gräfenhain

Faial

West of Pico, Faial is known as the Blue Island for its profusion of hydrangeas. With an area of 172 sq km (66 sq miles), it is the most cosmopolitan and nautical island of the Azores.

The first settlers were Portuguese and Flemish peasants, who came here in the second half of the 15th century, and a few ancient windmills still bear witness to this period. Faial was a consular town on the world's great maritime routes, and a port of call for British and American whalers until the 19th century; it has always been renowned for its role as a stopover island. In modern times it has served in turn as a coaling station for steamships, a telegraphic communications centre, a fuelling stop for Pan American clippers, and a naval base during the two world wars, and one of the ports used by the Allies at the time of the Normandy landings in 1944. Joshua Slocum, the first man to sail around the world single-handed, set out from Boston in a sloop in 1895 and called in at Horta; he was followed by other famous lone yachtsman such as Eric Tabarly, Sir Francis Chichester, Malinovsky and more.

Horta

A well-known stage on transatlantic yacht races, Horta nestles in a wide, sheltered bay in the southeast of the island. It has become the tradition for sailors to leave a mark of their passage here, by painting images or symbols of their ships on the dock walls. Every inch of space is covered by pictures, new ones painted over old ones, building up a mosaic of colour. Over time, the belief has developed that any passing boat unrecorded on this wall of fame will suffer some dreadful mishap, a superstition that encourages every yachtsmen to set to with paint and brush.

Marina

The yachting fraternity meets up at the **Café Sport** on the sea front, an institution established in 1918. The former owner, José Azevedo, known as Peter, features in many a traveller's tale. He departed this world in 2005 and the café is now run by his son. It serves many purposes: as a yachting club, meeting point and poste restante, a place to collect e-mail messages or to change money, to hitch a lift on a boat, to talk about seafaring or just to absorb the atmosphere. There is also an interesting **Scrimshaw Museum**, and whale-watching trips are organized.

Near the marina, the **Fort of Santa Cruz**, nowadays a hotel, was the theatre of many battles. It was occupied by Spanish troops in 1583 and attacked and seized in

1597 by Sir Walter Raleigh, who burnt down the main buildings and sacked the town.

Around Town

Northwest of the fort, the Convent of São Francisco (17th century) contains the **Museum of Sacred Art**, with a collection of 15th-century Flemish paintings. The church has a high altar of intricately carved and gilded wood.

Further north, above the port stands the big church of **São Salvador**, begun in 1680 by Jesuits. It has two magnificent panels of *azulejos* in the choir, illustrating biblical scenes.

Next door, the former Jesuit College was the last to be built in the Azores before the Jesuits were expulsed in 1760. It now houses the **Horta Museum**, which has sections on ethnography and painting, and a unique collection of miniatures made from fig-tree pith, cut from the heart of fig branches in winter before the sap rises. It is split into almost transparent slivers which are glued together to form animals, flowers, ships or houses.

On the heights, **Nossa Senhora do Carmo** church (1752), was restored after the 1998 earthquake.

Bay Views

The bay is closed to the south by **Monte da Guia**, a volcanic outcrop linked to the town by a short neck of land. From its slopes you get a splendid view over the rooftops. Around the edge, bordering the bay of **Porto Pim** where whaling boats once lay at anchor, stretches a long, beautiful beach of grey sand. Swimmers also appreciate **Almoxarife** beach, in another bay northeast of Horta.

Monte Carneiro forms a backdrop to the town. From here the view embraces on one side the Pico volcano, shrouded in clouds, and the sea, and on the other the beautiful **Flamengos valley**, scattered with houses (the name commemorates settlers from Flanders). Three ancient windmills stand silhouetted on a ridge to the north.

Around the Island

Travelling in a clockwise direction from Horta on the road that encircles the island, you will see several more fabulous views; first, over the village of **Feteira**, then beyond Castelo Branco, out over Varadouro bay. The village is known for its hot springs, with a temperature of 35°C (95°F).

Back on the main road, take the turn-off for **Praia da Fajã**. At the bottom of the cliffs, at the very end of the road, there's a lovely little beach of black sand, swept by the raging Atlantic breakers.

Just east of **Praia do Norte**, on the north coast, the **Costa Brava** viewpoint looks out over the sea and low-lying agricultural land from a height of some 320 m (1,050 ft). A short distance further, beside another observation platform, tables and seats have been carved out of the lava rock, making a quiet spot for a picnic with a commanding view of the ocean.

Several roads winding between hydrangea hedges, some of them 2 to 3 m high (6 to 10 ft), lead up to **Cabeço Gordo**, the volcano that gave birth to Faia. One of them reaches the upper crater, known as Caldeira, 2 km (3 miles) wide and 400 m (1,300 ft) deep. The bottom is marshy, forming a fascinating monochrome in green. It's extremely windy at the top of the crater and it can also be very chilly; if you plan to walk along the ridge, make sure you have warm clothing.

Capelinhos. One night in September 1957, a new island was born just off the westernmost point of Faial. After a violent earthquake, steam and ash shot up from the depths of the ocean, and two weeks later a cone 800 m (2,600 ft) in diameter and over 100 m (330 ft) high appeared at the spot. Then, as suddenly as it had wakened, the earth went back to sleep. The waves soon wiped the new island off the map, and the inhabitants of Faial thought things were back to normal. But in the following November, volcanic activity started up again. Another island appeared, not far from the first. Lava started to flow, tremors increased, smoke and gas rose up from the Caldeira, in the centre of the island. The inhabitants had to be evacuated. Month after month, the volcano—baptized Capelinhos—grew in size, finally joining itself to Faial by an isthmus of solidified lava, until it quietened down in October 1958. Today, the area is spangled with ash (140 million cu m were released). You can still see the ruins of some of the 300 houses that were destroyed, and the lighthouse abandoned on the cliff. If you decide to walk through the site, stick to the paths worn by other walkers, because it is difficult for the fragile vegetation to get a hold on this patch of land. In the village of Capelo, a small museum recounts in photographs the story of this unexpected addition to the Azores family.

istockphoto.com/Hafenmann

A wall of sizzling canna lilies echoes the rooftops of Lajes das Flores.

Huber/Grafenhain

Flores and Corvo

Many consider Flores to be the most beautiful of all the Azorean islands. Far to the west of the archipelago, some 600 km (370 miles) away from São Miguel, it was not discovered until 1452. The first Flemish settlers named it Flores in 1475, in tribute to its masses of flowers. The island was abandoned because of its isolated location, and it was not re-colonized until 1528, this time by the Portuguese. The landscape is extremely rugged, with deep valleys and numerous crater lakes among the banks of hydrangeas. Around the coast, waterfalls cascade over beetling cliffs down to the sea. A perfectly adequate mesh of minor roads links all the towns and villages, but there is no way of driving all round the island.

Santa Cruz das Flores

The principal town is Santa Cruz on the northeast coast, a convenient departure point for excursions by boat or car to, for example, the large cave Gruto dos Enxaréus on the east coast. But first, climb up to the viewpoint of **Pico das Cruzes** for a splendid view over the village.

South Coast

The coast road dips into several luxuriant valleys on the way to the port of **Lajes das Flores** in the south, the island's second-largest settlement, then crosses to the west coast and the village of **Lajedo**. From here, a pleasant footpath descends through woods to **Ponta das Cantarhinas**, a 30-minute walk. Offshore are several lava islets, beaten by crashing Atlantic waves in a mass of foam.

Continuing northwards, you'll see the great basalt columns of the **Rocha dos Bordões** looming over the road. Just after the turn-off for **Fajãzinha**, a dizzying panorama from the foot of the transmission tower encompasses the village enclosed in a mountain cirque, cascades draining off rainwater, and the jagged wave-swept shore. In the village itself there are two old watermills near the start of the footpath for **Fajã Grande** (which can also be reached by road). Right at the end of the road, between cliffs and mountains, sea and sky, a handful of houses cling to a flat ledge at **Ponta de Fajã Grande**. Above the village you can see traces of a mudslide that wiped out some of the homes.

There are several ways through the barren centre of the island back to Santa Cruz. Make sure you have time in hand to visit the lovely **crater lakes**: Lagoa Funda, ensnared at the bottom of a funnel whose rim is level with Lagoa Rosa; Caldeira Comprida and Lagoa Negra further north, at the foot of Flores's highest peaks, Pico dos Sete Pés, Morro Alto and Pico da Burrinha.

North Coast

The road north from Santa Cruz takes you to **Fajã de Ponta Ruiva**, a picturesque old village neatly fitted above the cliffs between terraced fields of corn. An unmarked footpath winds in hairpin bends down to the sea, bordered by plots of pumpkins and yams. Now and then through the trees you perceive sensational views of the coast, lava islands—one pierced by an arch—and Santa Cruz in the distance.

On the road to **Ponta Delgada** at the northern tip of Flores, hydrangea bushes form a delightful frame for views of the village, which is set on a peninsula. Out to sea is the brooding silhouette of Corvo. The road peters out in front of the Albarnaz lighthouse, 3 km (2 miles) west of Ponta Delgada. From here you can walk along the northeast coast by a footpath that takes you to Ponta da Fajã Grande in 3 to 4 hours. Offshore, you can make out the little isle of **Monchique** behind the larger **Maria Vaz**; it marks the westernmost point of Europe. In the old days, mariners used it as a reference to verify their position and calibrate their navigational instruments.

Corvo

Only 15 nautical miles from Flores, Corvo is the most northerly and smallest of the Azores, with an area of 17 sq km (7 sq miles). The crossing takes an hour or so in summer; the rest of the year, the sea approach is impracticable because of storms.

The first settlers arrived in the early 16th century. Antão Vaz, a native of Terceira, soon abandoned the island, as did a later group of men from Terceira led by the Barcelos brothers. Then Gonçalo de Sousa sent some of his cattle to graze on the island, accompanied by slaves. They were joined by inhabitants from Flores. For many years their only means of communication with Flores was by bonfire. Corvo, originally known as the Island of Sea Crows (Corvos Marinhos), now has fewer than 400 inhabitants, mostly fishermen and shepherds living in **Vila do Corvo**. This is the only village, set on the south side of the island on the lower slopes of a volcano. The long, red-roofed houses cluster around the small church of Our Lady of the Miracles.

The islanders are known for their good tempers; the tale is told of a priest who was so persecuted by his parishioners that he had to flee to Flores by night, in 1995.

The northern part of the island is one huge caldera 300 m (985 ft) deep and 2 km (1.5 miles) in diameter, with two small lakes at the bottom dotted with tiny islands.

FACTS AND FACETS

Azores High
The anticyclone, frequently mentioned in weather forecasts, consists of a region of high pressure centred over the Atlantic somewhere in the region of the archipelago. It is a thermal, as opposed to dynamic, anticyclone, formed by the cooling of the atmosphere over the continents in winter and the oceans in summer. It governs the general movement of the winds over all the seas of the northern hemisphere.

Architecture
The first of Portugal's great architectural periods that is also apparent in Madeira and the Azores was introduced when the house of Avis acceded to the throne in 1385, and reflects the country's opening up to outside influences.

The Manueline style developed from 1490 to 1540, borrowing elements from Arab and Far Eastern cultures in both structure and decoration. Named after Manuel I, the style featured twisted columns, marine and floral symbols, sails, ropes and knots, models of the celestial sphere (the king's emblem) demonstrating the movement of the stars, adorning façades and embellishing doorways and windows.

Another period began in 1640 after the Spanish were driven out of Portugal by John IV, first king of the Braganza dynasty. During the reign of his son, the exuberance of baroque became the fashion. Churches were decorated with riotously carved and gilded wood, and soon all monuments from the most grandiose to the least significant were clad in *azulejos*.

Azulejos
Of Hispano-Arab origin, and imported from Seville, *azulejos* (from the Arabic *al-zuleiq,* meaning "polished stone") were used as a decorative element across the whole of Portugal and the islands. Assembled in panels, the tiles generally illustrate scenes from daily life, or depict historical or religious subjects. Originally the tiles were decorated with geometrical or abstract designs, incised before firing and glazing. In the middle of the 16th century a new technique was discovered, based on majolica ware from Italy. Henceforth the designs were painted on a background of

Fireworks celebrate the New Year in the bay of Funchal.

white enamel. Under Spanish domination, there was a temporary return to geometrical patterns. The blue colour is predominant nowadays, though yellow tiles can also be found. The finest examples date from the end of the 17th century.

Festivals

The year begins with Carnival, when the streets throb to the sound of the samba brought from Brazil. Then comes Madeira's Flower Festival. After Easter, one procession follows hard upon the heels of another in the Azores. On the first Sunday, the Senhor dos Enfermos is celebrated, then Senhor Santo Cristo dos Milagres on the fifth Sunday, in Ponta Delgada, when huge crowds follow the statue of Christ along the streets strewn with azalea petals. In May and September the islanders celebrate Espírito Santo, the Holy Spirit, ending, in Terceira, with the *touradas a corda*. In this special kind of bullfight, a bull with a halter round its neck is released into the village streets. In June, Terceira celebrates the Festas Sanjoaninas. August brings a flurry of festivities both religious and maritime: a pilgrimage from São Vicente to Porto Santo, then to the church of Nossa Senhora do Monte, the week-long Festival of the Sea at Faial, the Whalers Festival at Pico, and so on. In autumn there's the grape harvest. The annual highlight is New Year's Eve with a spectacular fireworks display over the bay of Funchal, where the harbour is packed full of cruise ships and all the houses and buildings are lit up.

Romeiros

During Lent, groups of men, usually from the same parish, wander along the roads of the Azores for eight days, reciting prayers and psalms. They walk in single file, led by a "brother master", wearing cape and scarf, rosary in hand and leaning on a thick staff, travelling from oratory to chapel and covering an average of 40 km (25 miles) every day. This tradition began in the 16th century, at a time when natural disasters frequently overwhelmed the archipelago, and were intended to attract the grace of God by penitence. They continue today often in the form of thanks to the Virgin or a saint who has answered prayers.

Wines

The famous tipple happened by chance. The first vines, of malvasia or malmsey type, were brought to the island from Cyprus and Crete in the early years of colonization. By 1455, the renowned *vinho generoso* of Madeira, nurtured on rich volcanic soil, was being produced, and within a few decades it had found its way to the cellars of all the crowned heads of Europe. Other grapes were introduced to the island by the Jesuits, Sercial (similar to Riesling), Bual and Verdelho. However, it was not until the 18th century and the development of long distance navigation that the Madeira wine as we know it made its entry on the stage.

English ships en route for the Far East used to fill their holds with barrels of wine for bartering, as ballast and to quench the thirst of their crews. During his first voyage to the South Pacific in 1768, Captain Cook took aboard 10,000 litres (over 13,000 bottles). Sometimes the quartermasters overestimated their requirements and had to return their excess barrels when back on Madeira. And so it was observed that after several months at sea, the wine, which had been fortified with cane sugar alcohol to support the voyage, had improved. Marketed under the name "Wine Returned from India", it enjoyed a phenomenal success which resulted in a change in production methods after 1794.

Two hundred years later, the wine matures in the same way. After three months macerating in mahogany casks, the best vintages are mixed with wine alcohol to stop the fermentation, then transferred to barrels of American oak where they remain for a minimum of 20 years—some even for 150 years. All categories included, the annual production on Madeira is about 4 million litres of wine. They reach 18° or 20° proof.

istockphoto.com/Khochenkov

A whole wall full of beautifully packaged biscuits to dip in your Madeira wine.

Marc Michel

SHOPPING

Faithful to their ancestral traditions, the Madeira islanders greatly appreciate arts and crafts. Embroidery and wickerwork are the most prominent, but you'll also be tempted by the ceramics and, of course, bottles of wine, as well as fresh flowers, and pineapples from the Azores.

Where?

All the towns have souvenir shops in the region of the main square, near the church or the market place. Some, like the Casa do Turista de Funchal, between Avenida Arriaga and the sea front, stock a bit of everything. Others, like the Madeira Wine Company, are more specialized. For embroidery, visit Funchal's Instituto do Bordado and the little shops on Rua das Murças. The shopping centres generally have boutiques, too. Each village has shops selling its own local crafts.

Antiques

Portuguese and Chinese porcelain and old furniture are to be found in Funchal.

Ceramics

In the Azores, the pottery of Lago (a village on São Miguel), hand-painted with rather plain blue decoration, is of high quality. You can choose from plates, bowls, vases, teapots, and so on, anything you fancy. The pottery and porcelain in Madeira is usually brightly coloured. *Azulejos*, the traditional hand-painted tiles can be bought singly (with motifs of fish, flowers, whales, etc.) or in complete panels representing religious scenes, seascapes with boats, landscapes, and so on.

Needlecrafts

On Madeira, embroidery is still a living tradition: more than 20,000 people make their living from their skills with needle and thread. In the middle of the 19th century an English lady called Miss Elizabeth Phelps, convalescing in the island, commissioned some needlework from the local women, and they never looked back. Most of the designs, very finely executed, are floral, and you can buy any kind of table linen from serviettes to large tablecloths embroidered with the name of the island.

In the Azores, the women do embroidery and crochet bedspreads. Many island ladies knit heavy woollen sweaters and traditional bonnets complete with earflaps and pompons.

Natural Products

Tropical flowers (anthuriums, bird of paradise, orchids) are sold in the markets of Funchal and at Madeira airport. They can be specially packaged for the journey.

Delicious Azorean pineapples are packaged by the pair in cartons to facilitate transport. You'll also find honey and tobacco on São Miguel.

Scrimshaw

In the Azores, you can still find sperm whale teeth engraved with marine or hunting scenes, as carved by the whalers of ancient times. Scrimshaw was extremely popular in the United States and Bermuda in the early 20th century and was recognized as an art in its own right. Small objects and jewellery made from whalebone are also on sale. Check the origin before buying: in any case you will need an authorization to import it into your home country.

Souvenirs

In no particular order, leather belts, traditional musical instruments such as the *brinquinho*, a stick to which are attached little wooden puppets in local costume playing the cymbals. On Corvo, you can buy traditional wooden locks that may not keep out burglars but make unusual keepsakes. Graciosa makes a unique musical instrument, the *viola de arame* or *de terra*, a kind of guitar with heart-shaped decorations. On Faial, you may find decorative flowers made from fish scales, an art that perhaps originated with the nuns.

Wickerwork

The region around Camacha is the centre of a large wickerwork industry. You can see all kinds of objects in the making and take home chairs, armchairs, baskets, bookcases, hats and even wicker animals. They can be delivered to your hotel. Production is more limited in the Azores, where you'll find baskets, floor mats and various miniature objects.

Wine

Treat yourself to at least one bottle of Madeira wine, whether your preference goes to Sercial, Verdelho, Bual, Malvasia or the rare Terrantez. To educate your palate, go to the Madeira Wine Company or the Institute of Wine at Funchal for a tasting. In the shops, you'll see bottles of Madeira that do not carry any of the above-mentioned labels; this wine is probably made from *tinta negra mole*, a more resistant vine introduced to the island in the 19th century after an epidemic of phylloxera ravaged the vineyards. It is the most common and the least highly rated.

The wine on sale is never less than three years old, but the best are aged for five to ten years. Exceptional years are kept even longer, and anything older than 20 is bound to be a great vintage. If you want to keep something for a future special occasion, you could invest in the 1996 vintage, said to be one of the best years of the decade. To drink it in style, why not take home a crystal carafe and glasses to match, made on the mainland?

The Azores specialize in fruit liqueurs, made from pineapple, maracujá, bananas and other fruit.

Woodcarving

At Faial, white fig pith is finely sliced and assembled with glue to make ornaments. You will also find scale models of whaling boats and other objects in cedar wood on Terceira.

What to buy? An embroidered tablecloth; a fan to keep cool; a magazine rack or a shopping basket to hold some cheese and a sausage—and a few bottles of wine.

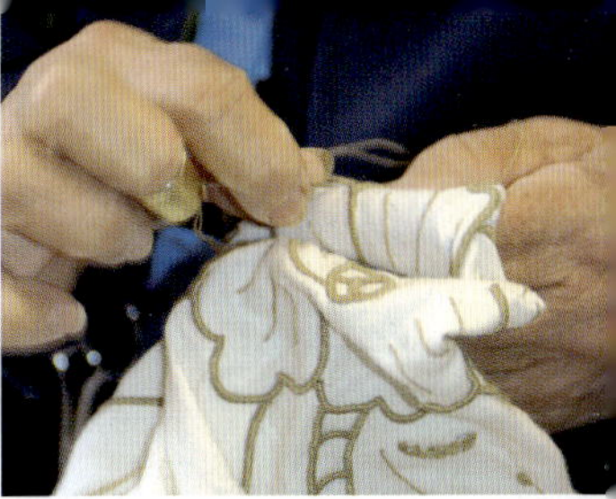
www.madeiratourism.org/DRTM

istockphoto.com/Mindor

istockphoto.com/Hills

Dominique Michellod

DINING OUT

Madeira and the Azores add local variations and recipes to Portuguese cuisine. While freshly caught fish, corn and vegetables cooked in olive oil with plenty of garlic form the basic diet, meat is also greatly appreciated. Most meals are accompanied by wine.

Starters

On Madeira, starters are known as *acepipes*. Soup is often served at the beginning of a meal—*sopa de tomate e cebola* (tomato and onion), *de legumes gratinada* (topped with a vegetable gratin), *caldeirada* (a fish soup, served with apples on Terceira), cress soup on Flores, *sopa de Espírito Santo* (made from bread, milk and cheese, flavoured with sorrel) throughout the Azores. Tomato or tuna salads are also popular.

Main Course

Boiled or stewed pork and beef are the favourite meats, but sometimes they are casseroled with wine and garlic. Rabbit stew is also common. Staple accompaniments are fried *milho* (corn flour), potatoes or yams *(inhames)*, and many dishes are served with corn bread. A traditional dish on Madeira, reserved for feast days and holidays, is *espetada*, chunks of beef sprinkled with coarse salt, skewered on a sprig of bay and grilled over a fire kindled with bay twigs. *Caldo verde* is a hearty mixture of black pudding and chorizo sausage served with cabbage and mashed potato. Tripe and beans is another typical dish. In the Azores, yam sausages and boiled beef *(cozido)* are popular. *Cozido das furnas*—meat, rice and vegetables sealed in an earthenware pot and steamed for eight long hours in the fumaroles of volcanic fissures—is well worth waiting for.

Fish

Salt cod, *bacalhao*, is simply grilled. Sardines, *salmonete* (red mullet), crayfish, shrimp and prawns are grilled, while octopus can be marinated in Pico wine. On Madeira, *espada*, swordfish, may also be breaded and fried; poached in wine with onions and tomatoes or simmered in a stew with beans, tomatoes and spices. Tuna steak *(bife de atum)* is often served grilled with onions and dressed with lemon or balsamic vinegar. Other fish and seafood on the menu are sole, eel, grouper, crab, spider crab and trout. Fresh clams are available on Santa Maria, and on Madeira don't miss the tasty *lapas*, skewered limpets with bacon.

istockphoto.com/Bogaerts

The edible fruit of the Swiss Cheese plant—banana ananas.

Dessert

São Jorge and Pico make well-known soft cheeses. Tarts and cakes are generously filled with cream; the famed *bolo de mel* are sweet, flaky pastries stuffed with molasses, cinnamon, fruit and walnuts. There is a wide range of exotic fresh fruit.

Drinks

There is a limited choice of local table wines. The fruity Atlantis rosé and dry Atlantis white are quite popular. A wide range of red and white wines from mainland Portugal is available, among them the renowned *vinho verde*, *dão* red or white and *pinhel* rosé. The Azores produce *vinhos do cheiro* (or *morangueros*), pleasantly fruity. Among the most appreciated are those of Caloura (São Miguel), Biscoitos (Terceira) and São Lourenço (Santa Maria). The best-known, however, is the *verdelho* from Pico.

Madeira is specifically produced as an aperitif or a dessert wine. Sercial is dry and light, pale in colour like dry sherry. Amber-coloured medium-dry Verdelho is fresh and subtle and perfect as an aperitif or with soup. Bual is fruity and full-bodied, served with cheese or dessert. Malvasia, the sweetest of all, is rich and honeyed, ideal with dessert or coffee.

Jinja, a relatively light cherry alcohol, is produced at Curral das Freiras on Madeira, while the Azores have invented various liqueurs: maracujá, pineapple, banana, blackberry, mandarin, coffee and milk. The locally distilled rum is called *aguardente*.

You'll find all the internationally known soft drinks, high-quality fruit juices, and sparkling or plain mineral waters bottled in Portugal, the Azores and at Porto Santo.

Coffee is usually served black and strong, called a *bica*. To obtain a white coffee, ask for *galão*.

SPORTS

From the warm waters of the Gulf Stream to their mist-wreathed volcanic peaks, the islands have something for everyone: sailing, diving, wind surfing, fishing, golf, tennis, hiking—you'll be spoilt for choice.

In the Water

As all of Madeira's beaches but one are covered in pebbles, it's hardly surprising that everyone flocks to the neighbouring island of Porto Santo to enjoy its magnificent stretch of fine gold sand, bathed by a limpid turquoise sea. But there are plenty of opportunities for swimming, whether in the sea, in natural pools, or in swimming pools. Quinta Magnolia, a veritable oasis of calm in the centre of Funchal, also has facilities for tennis and squash, besides a pool. In the Azores, there are several pleasant beaches of black or grey sand; they are not very extensive but are never crowded during the week. In some places the currents are dangerous.

Water skiing is practised everywhere, together with windsurfing and sailing, enhanced by reliable winds. Surfers appreciate the breakers around Santa Maria and São Miguel. Diving is excellent at Porto Santo, where the waters are particularly clear off the island of Baixo. There are several marine reserves in the Azores, where visibility can reach 25 m (80 ft) in summer. You can explore the grottoes of São Jorge and Flores, and the wreck of the *Dori* which sank near Ponta Delgada after World War II, and you can also swim with dolphins and sperm whales.

Deep-sea fishing is very popular off the shores of Madeira and the Azores. The species most commonly caught are grouper, barracuda, conger, bream, bass and mackerel. Big-game fishermen go in pursuit of swordfish, tuna, bonito and even shark. The Blue Marlin Tournament established a record catch of 540 kg (1,200 lb). Boats can be hired for four to six passengers for afternoon or day trips from June to October.

On São Miguel and Flores in the Azores, you can fish in crater lakes and rivers for trout, carp, perch and pike as long as you have a permit.

In the Mountains

On Madeira there is no shortage of footpaths, many of them the famous *levada* walks beside the irrigation channels. The trails sometimes cling to the sheer rockface, following the edge of a precipice or passing through low tunnels dripping with water. You need fine weather and good footwear. On the spot you can buy useful guides that explain the walks in detail and give ratings of the difficulty. The most popular are the ascent of Pico Ruivo, 3 hours from Pico do Arieiro, less than an hour from Achada de Teixeira; and the much shorter Balcões path from Ribeiro Frio.

In the Azores, the ascent of Pico is a classic, though the zone may be closed because of volcanic activity. It takes 3 to 4 hours, including a wearying stretch through cinders.

There are many possibilities for practising hang-gliding or paragliding on Madeira and Faial.

Other Sports

Tennis, squash and table tennis can be played in the hotels and local clubs. Several equestrian centres offer possibilities for riding: on Madeira and in the Azores at Terceira and São Miguel. Golf is a fast-growing sport: Madeira has two eighteen-hole courses, Porto Santo one and the Azores three (São Miguel and Terceira).

www.madeiratourism.org

istockphoto.com/Bogaerts

www.madeiratourism.org

www.madeiratourism.org

Airports

Both Madeira and its neighbour Porto Santo have an international airport, receiving flights from many destinations in Europe. Madeira airport is 23 km (14 miles) east of Funchal.

Porto Santo airport was opened in 1960. There are plenty of taxis to drive you into town within 10 minutes.

Each island of the Azores has its own airport, three of which have direct flights to Lisbon as well as other European destinations: Ponta Delgada on São Miguel (the main airport, also linked with Funchal), Lajes on Terceira and Horta on Faial.

At Madeira and Ponta Delgada airports, there are car-hire desks, restaurants, bars, souvenir shops, currency exchange, cash distributors, information, a post office and all the usual facilities.

Climate

On the same latitude as southern Morocco, Madeira is very mild all year round, cooler at altitude. The average temperature on the coast is 17°C (63°F) in winter and 23°C (73°F) in summer. In the mountains, it is frequently cloudy and the rain can be heavy, particularly between October and December. Spring is the best time to see the exuberant flora of the islands, autumn for the grape harvest. The sea temperature benefits from the passage of the Gulf Stream.

Though the name is associated with the anticyclone that regulates the appearance of the sun over western Europe, the Azores do not benefit from as sunny a climate as you may imagine. Depressions forming off the American coast, even in the middle of summer, cause a layer of cloud to form over the islands and drench them in fine, misty rain before heading off to continental Europe. The western islands are twice as wet as those in the east. The weather is very changeable, so much so that you can get a taste of all four seasons in one day. However, temperatures are mild, ranging from an average 14°C (57°F) in winter to 23°C (73°F) in summer, peaking at 27°C (80°F). In August, the sea temperature remains steady at 24°C (75°F).

Clothing

In summer, lightweight clothing, a swimsuit and sunglasses, comfortable shoes and a light sweater for walks at altitude will be adequate. A waterproof may be useful at any season, especially in the

Azores, but is absolutely indispensable in late autumn and winter. Certain restaurants, especially those in the luxury hotels, require more formal dress.

Communications

Letters and postcards take a few days to reach mainland Europe; they travel more rapidly if sent via *Correio Azul*, air mail.

International calls can be made from card-operated phone boxes. Dial 0044 for the UK, followed by the area code minus the initial zero, and the local number.

To call Madeira or the Azores from outside Portugal, dial:

Madeira: +351 291
São Miguel and
Santa Maria: +351 296
Terceira, Graciosa,
São Jorge: +351 295
Pico, Faial, Flores,
Corvo: +351 292

and the local number.

Currency

The Euro, divided into 100 cents. Coins: 1 to 50 cents, 1 and 2 euros; banknotes: 5 to 500 euros. Most credit cards are widely accepted, with a preference for Visa and American Express. These can also be used to withdraw money from cashpoints.

Driving

Island roads follow the contours of the land in an exhilarating series of bends, slopes, bridges and tunnels. Do not expect to go faster than an average 30–40 kph (18–25 mph). The asphalted and paved roads are generally in good condition, except on the Azores where the secondary roads often leave much to be desired.

Traffic is often dense in towns, and parking places are scarce. It is virtually impossible to park in Funchal, so use your hotel's shuttle service, a taxi or a bus to go there.

Before you set off to explore the island, try and get hold of a detailed map (those supplied by the car hire companies don't show all the roads). Most rental companies require drivers to be at least 23 or 25 years old, and to have been licence holders for more than 12 months. In July and August, it is prudent to reserve your car several days in advance.

Emergencies

For emergency help, dial 115.

Health

There are no special health precautions required. However, be careful of sunburn, especially in the Azores where the sun is often veiled. As the islands are part of the European Union, other EU citizens should carry a European Health Card, which ensures that costs are reimbursed if emergency treatment is necessary.

Holidays and Festivals

In addition to the following public holidays, there are numerous festivals and saint's days throughout the islands (see p. 74).

January 1	*New Year's Day*
April 25	*Liberty Day (The Carnation Revolution)*
May 1	*May Day*
June 1 (Azores)	*Independence Day*
June 10	*Birthday of Camões (poet)*
July 1 (Madeira)	*Discovery of Madeira*
August 15	*Feast of the Assumption*
October 5	*Republic Day*
November 1	*All Saints' Day*
December 1	*Restoration of Independence*
December 8	*Feast of the Immaculate Conception*
December 25	*Christmas*
December 26	*Boxing Day* (Madeira)

Moveable: Good Friday, Whit Monday, Corpus Christi.

Formalities

To enter Portugal, citizens of EU countries need only an identity card or passport. Passengers from EU countries may import the following goods, tax-paid: 800 cigarettes or 200 cigars or 1 kg tobacco products; 10 litres spirits over 22°, 20 litres spirits less than 22°, 90 litres wine and 110 litres beer. Passengers from non-EU countries may import, tax-free: 200 cigarettes or 50 cigars or 250 g tobacco products; 1 litre spirits over 22° or 2 litres of other alcoholic beverages of 22° or less, and 4 litres still wine and 16 litres beer; 50 g perfume and 250 ml eau de toilette.

Language

The official language is Portuguese, with an accent quite distinct from continental Portugal and littered with vocabulary specific to the islands. English is widely spoken in the Azores and to a lesser extent on Madeira.

Media

As well as the main Portuguese daily papers, Madeira and the Azores have several local papers. Foreign newspapers are available from many bookshops and kiosks. Virtually all the tourist hotels receive cable television, with in addition to the national channels (RTP1, RTP2, RTP Madeira and RTP Açores) several others including BBC World, EuroNews, EuroSport, CNN, NBC, and so on.

Opening Hours

Banks on Madeira open Monday to Friday 8.30 a.m.–3 p.m., sometimes Saturdays 9 a.m.–1 p.m. Some close for lunch. In the Azores, banks open Monday to Friday 8.30 a.m.–noon and 1.30–2.30 p.m. *Bureaux de change* open Monday to Saturday (9 a.m. –1 p.m., 2–7 p.m.).

Shops on Madeira open Monday to Friday 9 a.m.–1 p.m. and 3 p.m.–7 p.m., Saturdays 9 a.m. to 1 p.m. In the Azores, they open weekdays 9 a.m.–12.30 p.m. and 2–6.30 p.m., Saturdays to 1 p.m. However, on most of the islands, more and more shops and supermarkets stay open later in the evenings and even on Sundays.

Museums close on Mondays and bank holidays, and in many cases also on Saturdays and Sunday mornings.

Photography

The islanders will happily submit to being photographed if you ask them politely. Do not forget to take extra memory cards and your battery charger.

Time

Madeira keeps the same time as the UK and mainland Portugal: GMT in winter, GMT + 1 in summer. The Azores are one hour behind: GMT–1 in winter, GMT in summer.

Tipping

Service is generally included, but it is nevertheless usual to leave an extra tip equivalent to 5% or 10% of the total bill.

Security

Theft is infrequent and mugging virtually unknown, but it is still sensible to keep your car locked when you leave it parked.

Transport

From Funchal you can reach Porto Santo by plane (a 15-minute trip), advance booking essential; or by ferry every day except Tuesday in low season—for the timetable see:

www.portosantoline.pt

The Azores are well served by international flights or local flights from Funchal or Lisbon with TAP or SATA. Island-hopping packages are available, and there is an inter-island ferry:

www.transmacor.pt

It is easy to hire a car or motorbike on Madeira, a little less so in the Azores, where there are fewer international rental companies. It can be quite economical to hire a taxi for the day. The bus network is extensive though a bus ride will take longer than you might expect. Porto Santo has a minibus service running between Vila Baleira and the hotels.

Voltage

The electrical supply is 220 volts, 50 Hz. Plugs have two round pins.

General editor
Barbara Ender-Jones

English adaptation
Judith Farr

Proofreading
Lisa Costantini

Design
Karin Palazzolo

Layout
Luc Malherbe, Matias Jolliet

Photo credits
p. 1: fotolia.com/mountainguide (Madeira landscape)
p. 2: Huber/Gräfenhain (São Jorge cheese); istockphoto.com/Gough (lambs); /Spamer (cactus Funchal botanical garden); fotolia.com/Berru (restored mill, Faial, Azores)

Maps
JPM Publications,
Mathieu Germay

12, avenue William-Fraisse,
1006 Lausanne, Switzerland
information@jpmguides.com
http://www.jpmguides.com/

Printed in Switzerland
13092.00.5513
Weber/Bienne
Edition 2009–2010

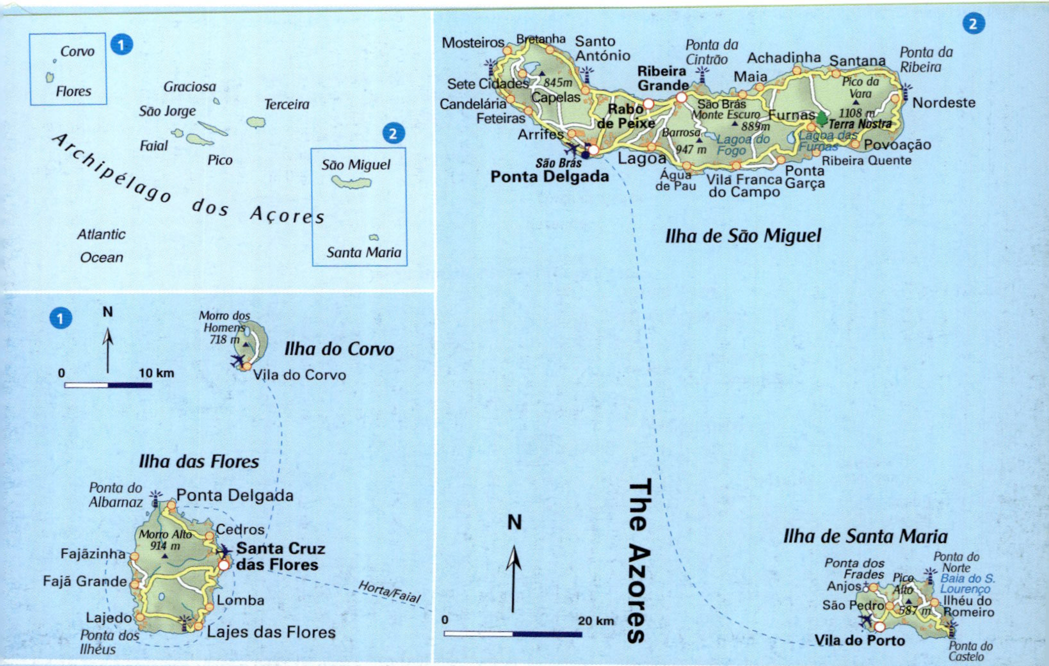
The Azores
Archipélago dos Açores
Atlantic Ocean
Corvo
Flores
Graciosa
São Jorge
Terceira
Faial
Pico
São Miguel
Santa Maria
1
2
N
0
10 km
Ilha do Corvo
Morro dos Homens 718 m
Vila do Corvo
Ilha das Flores
Ponta do Albarnaz
Ponta Delgada
Cedros
Morro Alto 914 m
Santa Cruz das Flores
Fajãzinha
Fajã Grande
Lomba
Lajedo
Lajes das Flores
Ponta dos Ilhéus
Horta/Faial
Ilha de São Miguel
Mosteiros
Bretanha
Santo António
Sete Cidades
845m
Candelária
Capelas
Feteiras
Arrifes
São Brás
Ponta Delgada
Rabo de Peixe
Ribeira Grande
Ponta da Cintrão
Barrosa
947 m
Lagoa
Água de Pau
São Brás
Monte Escuro
889m
Lagoa do Fogo
Vila Franca do Campo
Maia
Achadinha
Furnas
Lagoa das Furnas
Terra Nostra
Ponta Garça
Ribeira Quente
Santana
Pico da Vara
1108 m
Povoação
Ponta da Ribeira
Nordeste
20 km
Ilha de Santa Maria
Ponta dos Frades
Anjos
Pico Alto
587 m
São Pedro
Vila do Porto
Ponta do Norte
Baia do S. Lourenço
Ilhéu do Romeiro
Ponta do Castelo

The Azores

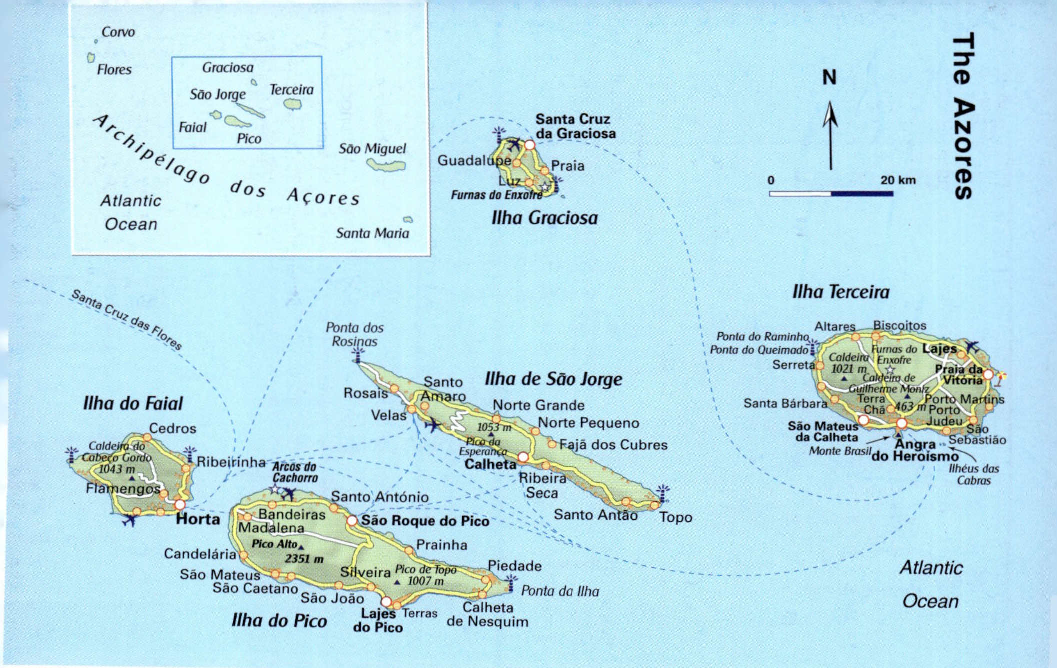

N
0
20 km
Corvo
Flores
Graciosa
São Jorge
Terceira
Faial
Pico
São Miguel
Archipélago dos Açores
Atlantic Ocean
Santa Maria
Santa Cruz da Graciosa
Guadalupe
Praia
Luz
Furnas do Enxofre
Ilha Graciosa
Ilha Terceira
Ponta do Raminho
Ponta do Queimado
Altares
Biscoitos
Caldeira 1021 m
Furnas do Enxofre
Lajes
Praia da Vitória
Serreta
Caldeira de Guilherme Moniz
Santa Bárbara
Terra Chã
463 m
Porto Martins
Porto Judeu
São Sebastião
São Mateus da Calheta
Monte Brasil
Angra do Heroísmo
Ilhéus das Cabras
Santa Cruz das Flores
Ponta dos Rosinas
Ilha de São Jorge
Rosais
Santo Amaro
Velas
Norte Grande
Norte Pequeno
1053 m
Pico da Esperança
Fajã dos Cubres
Calheta
Ribeira Seca
Santo Antão
Topo
Ilha do Faial
Cedros
Caldeira do Cabeço Gordo 1043 m
Ribeirinha
Flamengos
Horta
Arcos do Cachorro
Santo António
Bandeiras
Madalena
São Roque do Pico
Pico Alto
2351 m
Prainha
Candelária
Piedade
São Mateus
São Caetano
Silveira
Pico de Topo 1007 m
Ponta da Ilha
São João
Lajes do Pico
Terras
Calheta de Nesquim
Ilha do Pico
Atlantic Ocean